AF669054

Smart Success

Achieve Your Goals with Precision and Clarity

SMART REVALUATION®
DESIGN YOUR DAY

www.SmartRevaluation.com

Dream BIG, Plan SMART, and Succeed FAST.

Smart Success

Achieve Your Goals with Precision and Clarity

Professor Balu

MBA (IB)., MBA (IM)., M.Sc (Psy)., M.A (JMC).,

M.A (Eco)., M.A (Ps)., M.A (His)., M.A (Phi)., $\overline{Ph.D}$.,

PDAD., PDIT., MDSA., DIAE., PGDCA., CGP., WIPO.

Printed in India.

For more information, or to book an event, contact:
www.ProfessorBalu.com
Balu@ ProfessorBalu.com

Book design by: Smart Revaluation Publication
Cover design by: Smart Revaluation Publication

ISBN - Paperback: 978-81-972581-7-6

First Edition: January 2025

About the Author

Professor Balu is a distinguished Psychologist, Serial Entrepreneur, Motivational Speaker, and Business & Life Coach with over a decade of experience in industries and academics across multiple countries. A prolific academician and visionary, Professor Balu holds an impressive array of qualifications, including an MBA (International Business) from the University of East London, Singapore, and advanced degrees in MBA (Investment Management), Psychology, Journalism & Mass Communication, Economics, History, Philosophy, Political Science, and more.

Dr. G. Malathi, Assistant Professor of Management Studies at Gobi Arts & Science College, has over 21 years of teaching experience. She holds an MBA, M.Phil, and Ph.D. in Management and has authored "Total Quality Management". With 20+ research articles and 15 conference presentations, she continues to make significant contributions to management education and research.

Professor Balu and Dr. G. Malathi, both distinguished academicians and experts in their respective fields, have collaborated to bring this comprehensive guide on SMART goal setting. Combining their vast experience in psychology, management, and personal development, they have crafted a practical and insightful resource designed to help individuals set, pursue, and achieve their goals with clarity and confidence. Their shared passion for empowering others through structured strategies and research-based techniques makes this book an essential tool for anyone striving for success.

Acknowledgements

Writing this book has been an incredible journey, and I am deeply grateful to everyone who has supported and inspired me along the way.

First and foremost, I extend my heartfelt gratitude to all the individuals who have contributed to the evolution of SMART goal setting—thinkers, researchers, and practitioners who have shaped this powerful framework. Their insights and wisdom have paved the way for millions to achieve success with clarity and confidence.

A special thanks to my mentors, colleagues, and students who have shared their experiences, challenges, and triumphs in goal setting. Their stories have reinforced my belief in the power of structured, intentional action and have enriched the ideas presented in this book.

To my readers—whether you are an aspiring professional, a student, an entrepreneur, or simply someone striving for personal growth—this book is for you. Your ambition, curiosity, and willingness to embrace change are what make success possible. I hope these pages serve as a guide, a source of motivation, and a practical tool to help you turn your dreams into reality.

Lastly, I am grateful for the unwavering support of my family and friends. Their encouragement and belief in my work have been the driving force behind my dedication to sharing knowledge and empowering others.

Success is not just about setting goals; it's about setting the right goals and taking purposeful steps toward them. May this book help you chart a path to your greatest achievements.

— **Professor Balu**

Content

Chapter 1

GOAL

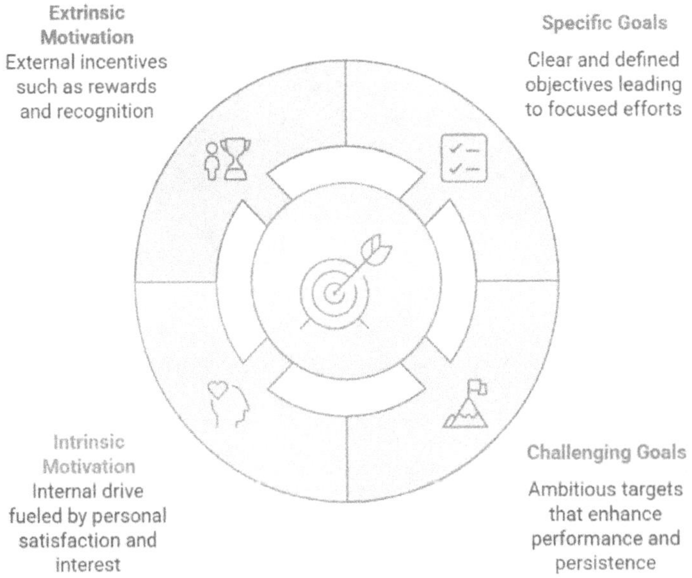

1. Understanding Goals

Understanding goals is a critical aspect of personal and professional development, as they provide direction, motivation, and a framework for measuring progress. The concept of goal-setting has evolved over time, drawing from various psychological theories and practical applications. The SMART criteria—Specific, Measurable, Achievable, Relevant, and Time-bound—has become a widely adopted framework that helps individuals formulate effective goals. This chapter will explore the significance of understanding goals, the historical context of goal-setting theories, and practical strategies for implementing them in everyday life.

The historical roots of goal-setting can be traced back to the early 20th century when psychologists began to study human motivation and behavior. One influential figure in this field was Edwin Locke, whose Goal-Setting Theory (1968) posited that specific and challenging goals lead to higher performance compared to vague or easy goals. Locke's research demonstrated that setting clear objectives not only enhances motivation but also fosters persistence and effort among individuals (Locke & Latham, 2002). This foundational theory laid the groundwork for subsequent developments in goal-setting methodologies.

In contemporary practice, the SMART criteria have emerged as a popular tool for structuring goals effectively. Each component of SMART plays a crucial role in ensuring that goals are well-defined and attainable. Specific goals clarify what needs to be accomplished; for instance, instead of saying "I want to get fit," a specific goal would be "I want to run a 5K." Measurable goals allow individuals to track their progress quantitatively, such as aiming to lose 10 pounds within three months. Achievable goals ensure that objectives are realistic given the individual's resources and constraints; setting an unattainable goal can lead to frustration and demotivation. Relevant goals align with broader life aspirations or values, making them more meaningful. Finally, Time-bound goals impose deadlines that create urgency and accountability (Doran, 1981).

Understanding the nuances of goal-setting is essential for effective implementation. Research indicates that breaking down larger objectives into smaller sub-goals can enhance motivation and make daunting tasks more manageable (Postan, n.d.). For example, if an individual aims to write a book, they might set sub-goals such as completing a chapter each month or dedicating specific hours each week for writing. This method not only provides a clear roadmap but also allows for celebrating small victories along the way.

Moreover, accountability plays a vital role in achieving goals. Sharing one's objectives with others can create a support system that encourages commitment and follow-through. Studies have shown that individuals who publicly commit to their goals are more likely to achieve them due to social pressure and encouragement from peers (Cialdini et al., 1991). This highlights the importance of community and relationships in the goal-setting process.

In addition to these strategies, it is crucial to regularly review and adjust goals based on progress and changing circumstances. Flexibility allows individuals to adapt their objectives as needed while maintaining focus on their overall aspirations. For instance, if someone encounters unforeseen challenges in their journey towards a career change, they may need to reassess their timeline or modify their approach without abandoning their ultimate goal.

The psychological aspect of understanding goals cannot be overlooked. The process of setting and pursuing goals can significantly impact an individual's self-esteem and overall well-being. Achieving goals fosters a sense of accomplishment and reinforces positive behaviors. Conversely, failing to meet objectives can lead to feelings of inadequacy or discouragement (Schunk & Zimmerman, 2008). Therefore, it is essential for individuals to cultivate resilience and a growth mindset—viewing setbacks as opportunities for learning rather than failures.

2. What are goals?

Goals are integral to human motivation and achievement, serving as the cognitive representation of desired outcomes that individuals strive to attain. The concept of goals has evolved significantly over time, with substantial contributions from psychology and organizational behavior. Historically, Edwin A. Locke and Gary P. Latham, pioneers in goal-setting theory, emphasized that specific and challenging goals lead to higher performance compared to vague aspirations or merely doing one's best (Locke & Latham, 2002). Their research indicates that goals direct attention and effort toward relevant activities, increase persistence, and foster the discovery of effective strategies for achieving desired results.

In psychological terms, a goal can be understood as a mental construct that represents a future state or outcome one wishes to achieve (Fishbach & Ferguson, 2007). This cognitive representation is not just about the end state but also involves the motivation to pursue it. Motivation can be intrinsic, stemming from the enjoyment of the task itself, or extrinsic, driven by external rewards (Lewin, 1935). This dual nature of motivation plays a crucial role in how effectively individuals set and pursue their goals.

The SMART goal-setting technique is a widely recognized framework that enhances the effectiveness of goal formulation. The acronym SMART stands for Specific, Measurable, Achievable, Relevant, and Time-bound. Each component serves a distinct purpose in ensuring that goals are clear and actionable. For instance, a vague goal like "I want to improve my health" can be transformed into a SMART goal: "I will exercise for 30 minutes five times a week for the next three months." This transformation not only clarifies the objective but also provides measurable criteria for success (Indeed.com, 2024).

The origins of the SMART framework can be traced back to Peter Drucker in the early 1980s when he introduced management by objectives (MBO) as a method for setting clear goals in organizations (ProductPlan, n.d.). Over time, this approach has been adapted for various contexts beyond business management, including personal development and education. The flexibility of the SMART framework allows it to cater to different needs while maintaining its core principles.

Research has shown that setting SMART goals significantly enhances commitment and performance. For example, studies indicate that individuals who establish specific goals are more likely to achieve them than those who set general objectives (Locke & Latham, 2002). Furthermore, feedback mechanisms are crucial; individuals who receive regular updates on their progress are more likely to stay motivated and adjust their strategies as needed.

In addition to its practical applications in personal and professional settings, the SMART technique aligns well with principles from positive psychology. Martin Seligman's work emphasizes the importance of setting realistic and meaningful goals that resonate with individual values and strengths (Luthans, 2002). This alignment fosters greater engagement and satisfaction in the pursuit of goals.

Casual anecdotes further illustrate the impact of goal-setting techniques like SMART. Consider Sarah, a marketing professional who felt overwhelmed by her workload. By applying the SMART criteria, she identified a specific goal: "I will complete my project report by next Friday by dedicating two hours each day to writing." This clarity not only alleviated her stress but also enabled her to track her progress effectively. As she met her daily writing targets, her confidence grew, demonstrating how structured goal-setting can lead to enhanced performance.

Another example is John, an aspiring runner who wanted to participate in a marathon. Initially daunted by the prospect of running 26 miles, he broke down his training into SMART goals: "I will run three times a week for 30 minutes each session for eight weeks." This approach allowed him to gradually build his stamina without feeling overwhelmed by the end goal.

The benefits of setting goals extend beyond individual achievement; they also foster collaboration and accountability within teams. In organizational settings, teams that adopt SMART goals often experience improved communication and alignment on objectives. For instance, during team meetings at a tech startup, members regularly review their SMART goals related to product development timelines. This practice not only keeps everyone on track but also cultivates a culture of support where team members celebrate each other's milestones.

Despite its advantages, goal-setting is not without challenges. One common pitfall is setting overly ambitious or unrealistic goals that can lead to frustration or burnout. It is essential for individuals and teams to regularly reassess their objectives to ensure they remain attainable and relevant given changing circumstances.

In conclusion, understanding what goals are and how they function within our lives is crucial for personal growth and achievement. The historical evolution of goal-setting theories combined with practical frameworks like SMART provides valuable insights into effective goal formulation. By embracing these principles, individuals can harness their motivation more effectively and navigate their paths toward success with clarity and purpose.

3. Difference between dreams and goals

The distinction between dreams and goals is a fundamental concept in personal development and achievement, especially within the framework of the SMART goal-setting technique. While dreams represent the aspirations and visions we hold for our future, goals serve as the actionable steps we take to turn those aspirations into reality. Understanding this difference is crucial for anyone looking to make meaningful progress in their personal or professional lives.

At its core, a dream can be described as an abstract idea or a desired outcome that exists primarily in one's imagination. Dreams are often characterized by their vagueness and lack of specificity; they provide a broad vision of what one hopes to achieve but do not inherently include a plan for how to get there. For example, someone might dream of becoming a successful author, but without specific actions or timelines, this dream remains an intangible aspiration. In contrast, a goal is defined as a specific target or objective that one actively works towards. Goals are concrete, measurable, and time-bound, making them essential for translating dreams into achievable outcomes (PlanPlus Online, n.d.; University of the People, n.d.).

Historically, the understanding of goals has been shaped by various psychological theories. Edwin Locke and Gary Latham's goal-setting theory posits that specific and challenging goals lead to higher performance than vague or easy ones (Locke & Latham, 2002). Their research emphasizes the importance of setting clear objectives that can be measured and evaluated over time. This aligns closely with the SMART criteria—Specific, Measurable, Achievable, Relevant, and Time-bound—which provides a structured approach to goal setting. For instance, instead of merely dreaming about writing a book, one could set a SMART goal: "I will write 500 words every day for the next three months to complete my manuscript." This goal is specific (500 words), measurable (daily word count), achievable (realistic output), relevant (aligned with the dream of becoming an author), and time-bound (three-month deadline).

The relationship between dreams and goals is often described as hierarchical; dreams inspire goals, while goals provide the roadmap to realize those dreams. Dreams can serve as motivational forces that push individuals toward their aspirations. They offer a vision of what could be possible and help individuals envision their ideal future. However, without actionable goals, dreams can remain just that—abstract ideas without any real-world impact (Creative Primer, n.d.; Success in Depth, n.d.).

Research supports the notion that individuals who set specific goals are more likely to achieve their desired outcomes compared to those who rely solely on their dreams. A study by Fishbach and Ferguson (2007) highlights how setting concrete goals can enhance motivation and focus. This is particularly relevant in contexts such as education or career development, where clear objectives can guide individuals through complex pathways toward success.

Casual stories often exemplify this distinction effectively. Take the story of Emily, who dreamed of traveling around the world. For years, she envisioned herself exploring different cultures and landscapes but never took any steps toward making it happen. One day, she decided to transform her dream into actionable goals: she created a savings plan to set aside money each month for her travels and researched potential destinations. By breaking her dream into smaller goals—such as saving $200 each month—Emily was able to turn her aspiration into a tangible plan. Eventually, she not only traveled but also experienced personal growth through her adventures.

Similarly, consider Mark's journey toward becoming a fitness coach. He had always dreamed of helping others achieve their health goals but felt overwhelmed by the enormity of his ambition. By setting specific fitness-related goals—such as obtaining certifications within six months and launching his coaching business within a year—Mark was able to create a structured path toward his dream career. His initial dream became more focused and actionable through goal setting.

The differences between dreams and goals extend beyond mere definitions; they encompass aspects such as accountability and resource allocation. Goals require commitment and effort; they often involve sacrifices in terms of time and resources (University of the People, n.d.). In contrast, dreaming is free from these constraints—one can dream endlessly without any investment or action required.

Moreover, while dreams can inspire creativity and imagination, they may also lead to disappointment if not pursued actively through goal setting. Many people maintain dreams throughout their lives without ever realizing them simply because they lack the framework necessary for achievement (PlanPlus Online, n.d.). The danger lies in allowing dreams to remain unfulfilled aspirations rather than transforming them into actionable plans.

In conclusion, understanding the difference between dreams and goals is essential for effective personal development. Dreams provide inspiration and vision for what one hopes to achieve in life; however, it is through setting specific goals that these dreams can be realized. The SMART framework serves as an invaluable tool for translating abstract aspirations into concrete actions that lead to meaningful outcomes. By recognizing that dreams are merely visions without actionable steps while goals are tangible targets requiring effort and commitment, individuals can better navigate their paths toward success.

4. Importance of setting clear goals

Setting clear goals is a vital component of personal and professional development, significantly influencing motivation, performance, and overall success. The importance of goal-setting has been extensively studied and documented in psychological literature, particularly through the lens of goal-setting theory pioneered by Edwin Locke and Gary Latham. Their research indicates that specific and challenging goals lead to higher performance levels compared to vague or easy objectives (Locke & Latham, 2002). This distinction highlights the necessity of clarity in goal setting, as it directly impacts an individual's ability to achieve desired outcomes.

The concept of goal clarity is essential for understanding its importance. Clear goals provide direction, enabling individuals to focus their efforts on specific tasks that contribute to their overall objectives. According to Locke and Latham (2006), clear goals help direct attention and effort toward activities that are relevant to achieving those goals while minimizing distractions from non-essential tasks. This focused approach enhances motivation by creating a sense of purpose; individuals are more likely to engage in behaviors that align with their goals when they understand what is expected of them.

Research supports the assertion that clear goals enhance performance across various contexts. A meta-analysis conducted by Klein et al. (1999) reviewed 83 independent studies on goal setting and job performance, revealing that employees who set specific, challenging goals exhibited a 16% improvement in performance compared to those without such goals. This improvement can be attributed to several mechanisms outlined in goal-setting theory, including direction, effort, persistence, and strategy development (Locke & Latham, 1990). When individuals have clear objectives, they are more likely to exert greater effort and persist in the face of challenges, ultimately leading to enhanced performance.

In addition to improving performance, setting clear goals also fosters a sense of accountability. When individuals articulate their objectives clearly, they create a framework for measuring progress and evaluating success. This accountability encourages individuals to take ownership of their actions and decisions, reinforcing their commitment to achieving their goals (Davis & Stazyk, 2015). For example, a student who sets a clear goal of achieving a specific grade in a course is likely to monitor their progress regularly and adjust their study habits accordingly.

The psychological benefits of goal setting extend beyond mere performance metrics. Research by Sheldon and Kasser (1998) found that individuals who set personal goals aligned with their intrinsic values experienced higher levels of well-being and a greater sense of purpose. This alignment between goals and personal values contributes to overall life satisfaction and mental health. Furthermore, Schunk and Zimmerman (2007) demonstrated that clear goals can reduce stress by providing individuals with a sense of control over their tasks. When people know what they need to achieve and have a plan in place, they are less likely to feel overwhelmed by their responsibilities.

Casual anecdotes often illustrate the transformative power of setting clear goals. Consider the story of Alex, an aspiring musician who dreamed of performing at local venues but struggled with self-doubt and procrastination. After attending a workshop on goal setting, Alex decided to establish specific targets: he would practice guitar for one hour each day and book at least one gig per month. By breaking down his dream into actionable steps, Alex not only improved his skills but also gained confidence as he began performing regularly. This journey underscores how clarity in goal setting can propel individuals toward realizing their aspirations.

Similarly, Sarah's experience as a project manager exemplifies the importance of setting clear goals within organizations. Faced with a complex project involving multiple stakeholders, Sarah implemented SMART goals for her team: each member was assigned specific tasks with measurable outcomes and deadlines. This clarity not only helped team members understand their roles but also facilitated better collaboration as everyone worked toward shared objectives. As a result, the project was completed ahead of schedule with high-quality outcomes—demonstrating how clear goal setting can enhance team performance.

Moreover, the significance of clarity in goal setting extends beyond individual or team contexts; it plays a crucial role in organizational success as well. Companies that establish clear organizational goals often witness improved employee engagement and productivity. A study by Rainey and Jung (2015) highlighted that organizations with well-defined objectives experience lower levels of role ambiguity among employees. When employees understand what is expected of them within the larger organizational framework, they are more likely to contribute effectively toward achieving those goals.

Despite the numerous benefits associated with setting clear goals, challenges can arise if those goals are not realistic or attainable. Setting overly ambitious targets may lead to frustration or burnout when individuals struggle to meet expectations (Locke & Latham, 2006). Therefore, it is essential for individuals and organizations alike to ensure that their goals are not only specific but also achievable within the given context.

In conclusion, the importance of setting clear goals cannot be overstated; they serve as essential tools for enhancing motivation, performance, accountability, and overall well-being. The research surrounding goal-setting theory provides robust evidence supporting the notion that specific and challenging objectives lead to improved outcomes across various domains—be it personal aspirations or organizational achievements. By adopting frameworks such as SMART goal setting—Specific, Measurable, Achievable, Relevant, Time-bound—individuals can create actionable plans that transform abstract dreams into tangible realities. As illustrated through anecdotes from both personal journeys and professional experiences, clarity in goal setting empowers individuals and teams alike to navigate their paths toward success effectively.

Your Business / Carrier Goals

Your Health Goals

Your Relationship Goals

Your Financial Goals

Your Spiritual / Mental Health Goals

Chapter 2

SMART

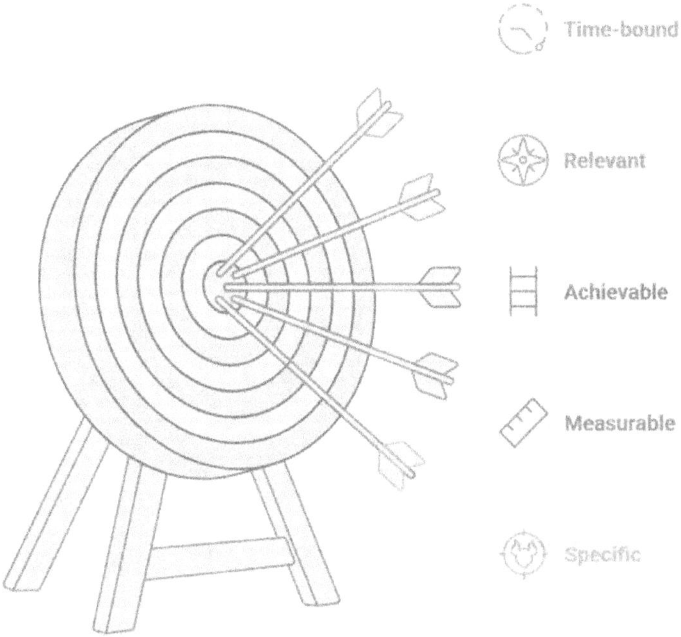

5. History and development of the SMART framework

The SMART framework, an acronym for Specific, Measurable, Achievable, Relevant, and Time-bound, has become a foundational tool for effective goal-setting across various domains, including business, education, and personal development. Its history traces back to the early 1980s when George T. Doran, a consultant and former director of corporate planning for Washington Water Power Company, introduced the concept in his 1981 paper titled "There's a S.M.A.R.T. Way to Write Management's Goals and Objectives" published in Management Review (Doran, 1981). Doran's motivation for developing this framework stemmed from the observation that many organizational goals were often vague and lacked the clarity necessary for meaningful impact. He proposed that goals should be articulated in a way that made them actionable and measurable, thereby transforming abstract aspirations into tangible targets.

Doran's original formulation of the SMART criteria included five elements: Specific, Measurable, Assignable (or Achievable), Realistic (or Relevant), and Time-related. Each component was designed to provide a clear structure for setting goals that could guide individuals and organizations toward successful outcomes. For instance, specificity eliminates ambiguity by clearly defining what is to be achieved, while measurability allows for tracking progress and evaluating success. The assignable aspect ensures that responsibilities are clearly defined, making it easier to hold individuals accountable for their contributions (Doran, 1981). This initial framework was pivotal in establishing a structured approach to goal-setting that resonated with managers seeking to enhance productivity and performance.

The late 1980s marked a significant shift in the business landscape as organizations began to seek more effective methodologies for performance measurement and goal setting. During this period, the SMART framework gained traction as a practical tool for managers aiming to implement structured goal-setting strategies. A study published in Management Review in 1981 revealed that organizations employing formalized goal-setting strategies experienced productivity increases of up to 50% compared to those without such frameworks (Vorecol, 2024). This compelling evidence contributed to the widespread adoption of SMART goals across various sectors.

As the SMART framework evolved over the years, it underwent various adaptations and reinterpretations. While Doran's original formulation included "Assignable," many modern interpretations have shifted to "Achievable" or "Attainable." This change reflects a broader understanding of goal-setting that emphasizes not only the importance of setting realistic targets but also ensuring that they are within reach given available resources (PlanPlus Online, n.d.). Additionally, some authors have expanded the acronym to include supplementary letters such as "S" for "Self-defined" or "R" for "Results-focused," further enriching its applicability across different contexts (Vorecol, 2024).

By the early 2000s, interest in SMART goals surged as research indicated that only about 3% of the population engaged in consistent goal-setting practices. However, those who did were found to be ten times more successful in achieving their desired outcomes (Vorecol, 2024). This stark contrast underscored the significance of structured goal-setting methodologies like SMART in enhancing individual performance and organizational effectiveness.

The impact of SMART goals is further illustrated through various case studies and anecdotal evidence from organizations that have implemented this framework. For example, a tech company facing declining productivity introduced SMART goals to redefine its project management approach. By establishing clear objectives—specific tasks with measurable outcomes—the company reported a remarkable increase in project completion rates within just one quarter (Vorecol, 2024). Such success stories highlight how adopting SMART criteria can lead to transformative results by fostering accountability and engagement among employees.

In addition to enhancing performance within organizations, SMART goals have also been shown to improve individual motivation and satisfaction. Research conducted by the Dominican University of California found that individuals who wrote down their goals were 42% more likely to achieve them compared to those who did not (Vorecol, 2024). Furthermore, incorporating accountability measures—such as sharing goals with friends or colleagues—nearly doubled success rates. These findings emphasize the psychological benefits associated with clear goal-setting practices.

The evolution of SMART goals has also been influenced by technological advancements and changing workplace dynamics. As organizations increasingly embrace data analytics and digital tools for performance tracking, the application of SMART criteria has expanded beyond traditional settings. Companies now utilize software platforms to set real-time objectives and monitor progress against established benchmarks (Vorecol, 2024). This integration not only empowers employees to take ownership of their objectives but also aligns individual performance with broader organizational strategies.

Despite its widespread popularity and proven effectiveness, critics argue that the SMART framework may not always be suitable for every context or individual. Some scholars suggest that overly rigid adherence to specific criteria can stifle creativity and limit innovative thinking (PlanPlus Online, n.d.). Others contend that while clarity is essential for effective goal setting, flexibility is equally important; individuals should feel empowered to adapt their goals as circumstances change.

In conclusion, the history and development of the SMART framework reflect an ongoing evolution in our understanding of effective goal-setting practices. From its inception by George Doran in 1981 as a response to vague organizational objectives to its current status as a foundational tool for performance management across diverse sectors, SMART goals have proven their value in enhancing clarity, accountability, and achievement. As organizations continue to navigate complex environments marked by rapid change and uncertainty, the principles underlying SMART criteria remain relevant—offering a structured approach that empowers individuals and teams alike to pursue their aspirations with purpose and focus.

6. Understanding each component: Specific, Measurable, Achievable, Relevant, Time-bound

The SMART framework, which stands for Specific, Measurable, Achievable, Relevant, and Time-bound, is a powerful tool for effective goal-setting that has gained widespread adoption in various fields, including business, education, and personal development. Understanding each component of this framework is crucial for individuals and organizations aiming to set clear and actionable goals that lead to successful outcomes. The history of the SMART framework dates back to 1981 when George T. Doran introduced it in his article "There's a S.M.A.R.T. Way to Write Management's Goals and Objectives," published in Management Review (Doran, 1981). His work laid the foundation for structured goal-setting practices that have since evolved and adapted to meet the needs of diverse contexts.

Specific is the first component of the SMART framework and emphasizes the necessity of clarity in goal formulation. A specific goal answers fundamental questions about what is to be achieved, why it is important, and how it will be accomplished. For instance, instead of stating a vague goal like "I want to get fit," a specific goal would be "I will join a gym and work out three times a week for at least 30 minutes each session." This specificity eliminates ambiguity and provides a clear direction for action (Asana, 2024). Research has shown that specificity in goal-setting significantly increases the likelihood of success; Locke and Latham (2002) found that specific goals lead to higher performance than general ones. This specificity not only clarifies the desired outcome but also helps individuals focus their efforts on relevant tasks.

The second component, Measurable, relates to the ability to track progress toward achieving the goal. A measurable goal incorporates quantifiable criteria that allow individuals to assess their advancement. For example, rather than saying "I want to save money," a measurable goal would state "I will save $200 each month for six months." This allows individuals to monitor their savings progress and adjust their strategies if necessary (Indeed.com, 2024). The importance of measurability is supported by research indicating that tracking progress enhances motivation and commitment (Schunk & Zimmerman, 2008). By establishing clear metrics for success, individuals can celebrate small wins along the way, which fosters a sense of accomplishment and encourages continued effort.

The third component of SMART goals is Achievable. This aspect emphasizes setting realistic goals that are attainable given available resources and constraints. While goals should be challenging enough to promote growth, they must also be grounded in reality; setting unattainable goals can lead to frustration and disengagement (PlanPlus Online, n.d.). For example, if someone aims to run a marathon but has never run more than a mile before, an achievable goal would be "I will run a 5K within three months" rather than jumping straight into marathon training. Research by Locke and Latham (2006) highlights that achievable goals foster persistence and effort because individuals feel empowered by their ability to succeed. This balance between challenge and attainability is critical for maintaining motivation over time.

Relevant is the fourth component of the SMART framework, which underscores the importance of aligning goals with broader life objectives or organizational missions. A relevant goal ensures that what one aims to achieve resonates with personal values or contributes meaningfully to larger objectives. For instance, an individual might set a goal to improve public speaking skills because they aspire to advance in their career where effective communication is key (Atlassian, n.d.). The relevance of goals not only increases motivation but also enhances commitment; when individuals see how their goals fit into their overall life plans or professional aspirations, they are more likely to invest time and energy into achieving them (Schunk & Zimmerman, 2008).

The final component of SMART goals is Time-bound, which emphasizes the necessity of setting deadlines for achieving objectives. A time-bound goal creates a sense of urgency that can enhance motivation and focus efforts toward completion. For example, instead of stating "I want to write a book," a time-bound goal would specify "I will complete my book manuscript by December 31st." This deadline encourages consistent progress and helps individuals prioritize tasks effectively (Asana, 2024). Research indicates that deadlines can significantly improve performance by creating accountability; when individuals know they have a finite amount of time to achieve their goals, they are more likely to stay committed (Locke & Latham, 2002).

Casual stories often illustrate how these components come together in practice. Take the example of Maria, who wanted to improve her fitness level. Initially, she had a vague aspiration: "I want to get healthier." However, after learning about SMART goals from a workshop at her workplace, she transformed her aspiration into a clear objective: "I will join a local gym by March 1st and attend three classes each week for three months." By making her goal specific (joining a gym), measurable (three classes per week), achievable (based on her current schedule), relevant (aligning with her desire for better health), and time-bound (three-month timeframe), Maria set herself up for success. As she tracked her attendance and celebrated small milestones—like increasing her stamina—she remained motivated throughout her fitness journey.

Similarly, consider John's experience as a project manager tasked with improving team productivity. Initially overwhelmed by vague expectations from upper management regarding project outcomes, he decided to implement SMART goals within his team. He articulated specific objectives such as "We will complete

Project X by July 15th with at least five team members contributing weekly updates." By clarifying expectations through specificity while ensuring measurability (weekly updates), achievability (realistic workload), relevance (aligned with company objectives), and time constraints (July deadline), John fostered an environment where team members felt empowered and accountable.

In conclusion, understanding each component of the SMART framework—Specific, Measurable, Achievable, Relevant, and Time-bound—is essential for effective goal-setting practices. Each element plays a critical role in enhancing clarity, motivation, accountability, and ultimately success in achieving desired outcomes. By applying these principles across personal aspirations or organizational objectives alike, individuals can create structured pathways toward realizing their ambitions while fostering engagement along the way.

Chapter 3

The Psychology of Goal Setting

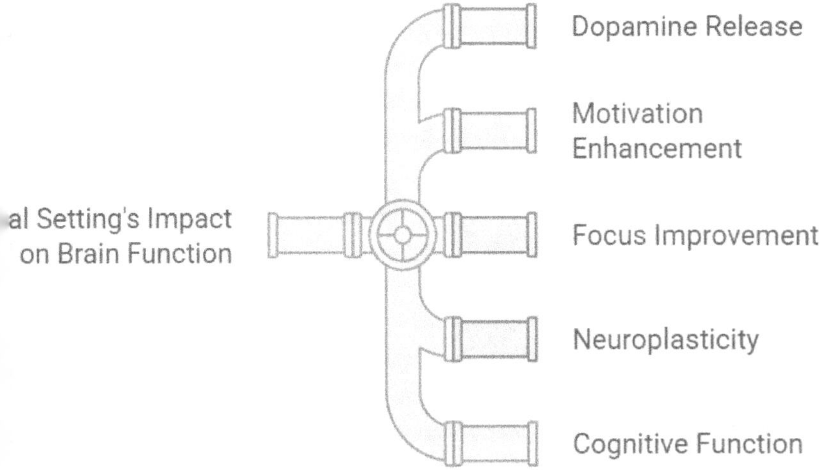

7. How goals affect the brain (dopamine, motivation, focus)

The relationship between goal setting and brain function is a fascinating area of study that highlights the profound impact that setting clear, structured objectives can have on motivation, focus, and overall cognitive performance. The SMART goal-setting technique—Specific, Measurable, Achievable, Relevant, and Time-bound—serves as a framework that not only enhances goal attainment but also influences the neurological processes associated with motivation and achievement. Understanding how goals affect the brain involves exploring the roles of neurotransmitters like dopamine, the mechanisms of neuroplasticity, and the psychological benefits of focused goal-directed behavior.

The Role of Dopamine in Goal Setting

Dopamine is often referred to as the "feel-good" neurotransmitter due to its association with pleasure and reward. It plays a crucial role in motivation and reinforcement learning. When individuals set goals and achieve them, dopamine is released in the brain, creating a sense of satisfaction and reinforcing the behavior that led to that achievement (Schultz, 2002). This biochemical reward system encourages individuals to pursue further goals, creating a positive feedback loop that enhances motivation.

Research has shown that setting challenging yet attainable goals can significantly increase dopamine levels. For instance, a study published in Behavioral and Cognitive Neuroscience Reviews indicated that individuals who set specific and ambitious goals experienced heightened dopamine release compared to those who set vague or easily achievable objectives (Top Stack Group, 2024). This increase in dopamine not only boosts motivation but also enhances focus and cognitive function, allowing individuals to concentrate better on tasks related to their goals.

Neuroplasticity: Rewiring the Brain for Success

Neuroplasticity refers to the brain's ability to reorganize itself by forming new neural connections throughout life. This phenomenon is particularly relevant in the context of goal setting. When individuals engage in goal-directed behavior, their brains adapt by strengthening pathways associated with those behaviors (Cohen et al., 2016). A landmark study involving multiple sclerosis patients demonstrated that those who set ambitious wellness goals reported fewer symptoms and improved health outcomes compared to those who did not set goals (Top Stack Group, 2024). This suggests that goal setting can lead to structural changes in the brain that enhance overall functioning.

The process of neuroplasticity is facilitated by the engagement of various brain regions during goal pursuit. The amygdala, responsible for emotional processing, evaluates the importance of a goal, while the frontal lobe—associated with problem-solving—helps define and strategize toward achieving it (Top Stack Group, 2024). When these areas work in tandem, they enable individuals to navigate challenges effectively and maintain focus on their objectives.

Motivation and Focus: The Psychological Benefits of Goal Setting

Setting clear goals not only influences brain chemistry but also enhances psychological factors such as motivation and focus. Research indicates that specific and challenging goals direct attention toward relevant tasks while minimizing distractions (Locke & Latham, 2002). This focused attention is critical for maintaining sustained effort over time. A meta-analysis published in Psychological Bulletin found that specific goals lead to higher performance than vague or easy ones because they mobilize effort and increase persistence (Locke & Latham, 2006).

Casual anecdotes often illustrate these principles effectively. Consider Sarah, a university student aiming to improve her academic performance. Initially overwhelmed by her coursework, she decided to apply the SMART framework by setting specific goals: "I will study for two hours every weekday evening for my upcoming exams." By establishing measurable criteria for success and a clear timeline, Sarah was able to focus her efforts more effectively. As she achieved her weekly study targets, she experienced a boost in confidence—an effect amplified by dopamine release—which further motivated her to continue her efforts.

Similarly, John's experience as a sales manager showcases how goal setting can enhance team performance. Faced with declining sales numbers, he implemented SMART goals for his team: "Each team member will increase their sales by 15% over the next quarter." By establishing specific targets and providing regular feedback on progress, John fostered an environment where team members felt accountable for their contributions. As they achieved their milestones, dopamine-driven rewards reinforced their motivation to strive for even greater success.

Challenges and Considerations

While goal setting has numerous psychological benefits, it is essential to recognize potential pitfalls associated with overly rigid or unrealistic goals. Research has indicated that when individuals set excessively ambitious targets without adequate support or resources, it can lead to feelings of failure or frustration (Forbes Books Authors, 2024). This highlights the importance of ensuring that goals are not only challenging but also achievable within the given context.

Moreover, focusing solely on outcome-based goals can sometimes detract from intrinsic motivation—the inherent satisfaction derived from engaging in an activity for its own sake (Ryan & Deci, 2000). Balancing extrinsic rewards associated with goal achievement (such as recognition or financial incentives) with intrinsic motivations is crucial for sustaining long-term engagement and well-being.

The psychology of goal setting reveals how structured approaches like SMART can significantly enhance motivation and cognitive performance through biochemical changes in the brain. Dopamine plays a central role in reinforcing behaviors associated with goal attainment while neuroplasticity allows for structural adaptations that optimize performance. By understanding these mechanisms and applying effective goal-setting strategies across personal aspirations or organizational objectives alike, individuals can create pathways toward realizing their ambitions while fostering engagement along the way.

8. The role of visualization and affirmation

The role of visualization and affirmation in goal setting is a dynamic interplay of cognitive and emotional processes that significantly enhances the effectiveness of achieving personal and professional objectives. Both techniques serve as powerful tools within the SMART goal-setting framework, which emphasizes the importance of setting Specific, Measurable, Achievable, Relevant, and Time-bound goals. By understanding how visualization and affirmation work together, individuals can harness their potential to foster motivation, enhance focus, and ultimately achieve their desired outcomes.

The Science Behind Visualization

Visualization is a mental technique that involves creating vivid mental images of desired outcomes or experiences. This practice has its roots in psychological theories and has been widely adopted in various fields, including sports psychology, therapy, and personal development. Research has shown that visualization activates the same neural pathways in the brain as actual physical practice (Cumming & Williams, 2012). For instance, a study published in The Journal of Sports Sciences found that athletes who engaged in visualization exercises demonstrated improved performance compared to those who did not (Taylor & Wilson, 2005). This phenomenon occurs because visualizing success helps to reinforce the neural connections associated with the actions required to achieve that success.

The effectiveness of visualization lies in its ability to enhance motivation and focus. When individuals visualize their goals, they create a mental representation of what success looks like. This process not only clarifies their objectives but also instills a sense of confidence and determination. A study conducted by Pham and

Taylor (1999) revealed that participants who visualized their goals were more likely to pursue them vigorously than those who did not engage in visualization. By mentally rehearsing the steps needed to achieve their goals, individuals can reduce anxiety and increase self-efficacy, making them more likely to take action.

The Power of Affirmations

Affirmations are positive statements that individuals repeat to themselves to reinforce their beliefs and intentions. The psychological mechanism behind affirmations is rooted in cognitive-behavioral principles; by consistently affirming positive beliefs about oneself, individuals can challenge and replace negative thought patterns (Seligman et al., 2006). Research indicates that affirmations can lead to increased motivation, reduced stress levels, and improved performance when used effectively (Schmeichel & Martens, 2005).

In the context of goal achievement, affirmations help clarify intentions and align daily actions with aspirations. For example, if an individual's goal is to advance in their career, an effective affirmation might be: "I am confidently taking steps every day to reach my professional goals." This statement not only reinforces the individual's commitment but also serves as a reminder of the actions needed to achieve success. Studies have shown that affirmations can significantly enhance self-regulation and persistence when pursuing long-term goals (Creswell et al., 2007).

Combining Visualization with Affirmations

The synergy between visualization and affirmations amplifies their individual effects on goal achievement. When individuals visualize their success while repeating affirmations, they create a powerful mental framework that reinforces belief in their capabilities. This combined approach engages both the cognitive and emotional aspects of goal pursuit.

For instance, when preparing for a significant presentation at work, an individual might visualize themselves confidently delivering their speech while simultaneously repeating affirmations such as "I am an effective communicator." This dual process not only enhances confidence but also activates neural pathways associated with successful performance (Cumming & Williams, 2012). By vividly imagining themselves succeeding while reinforcing positive beliefs through affirmations, individuals can create a compelling mental image that motivates them to take action.

Practical Applications: Stories of Success

Casual anecdotes often illustrate how visualization and affirmation can transform aspirations into reality. Consider the story of Emily, an aspiring entrepreneur who dreamed of launching her own business. Initially overwhelmed by self-doubt and uncertainty about her abilities, she decided to incorporate visualization and affirmation into her daily routine. Each morning, Emily would spend ten minutes visualizing herself successfully running her business—imagining interactions with satisfied customers and celebrating milestones with her team. Alongside this practice, she repeated affirmations such as "I am capable of achieving my entrepreneurial dreams." Over time, Emily noticed a significant boost in her confidence and motivation. As she took actionable steps toward her goal—researching her market and developing a business plan—she felt empowered by the mental imagery she had created.

Similarly, John's journey as a competitive athlete showcases the effectiveness of combining these techniques. Preparing for an important race, John utilized visualization by picturing himself crossing the finish line ahead of his competitors while feeling strong and energized. He paired this practice with affirmations like "I am strong; I will perform my best today." This combination not only helped him maintain focus during training but also reduced pre-race anxiety. On race day, John's mental preparation paid off as he achieved a personal best time.

Challenges and Considerations

While visualization and affirmation are powerful tools for goal achievement, it is essential to approach them with realistic expectations. Some individuals may find it challenging to fully engage in these practices due to deeply ingrained negative beliefs or past experiences of failure. In such cases, it may be beneficial to gradually build confidence through smaller achievements before tackling larger goals (Seligman et al., 2006). Additionally, consistency is key; regular practice of both techniques is necessary for them to be effective.

Moreover, it is crucial for individuals to ensure that their goals are aligned with their values and aspirations when using visualization and affirmation techniques. Engaging in practices that do not resonate personally may lead to feelings of disconnection or lack of motivation (Ryan & Deci, 2000). Therefore, taking time to reflect on what truly matters can enhance the effectiveness of these methods.

The role of visualization and affirmation in goal setting is significant; both techniques harness cognitive processes that enhance motivation and focus while reinforcing positive beliefs about oneself. By integrating these practices into the SMART goal-setting framework—where goals are Specific, Measurable, Achievable, Relevant, and Time-bound—individuals can create powerful pathways toward achieving their aspirations. The scientific research supporting these techniques underscores their effectiveness in promoting success across various domains. As illustrated through personal stories of triumph over self-doubt and obstacles, visualization and affirmation serve as invaluable tools for anyone seeking to turn their dreams into reality.

9. Overcoming procrastination and self-doubt

Overcoming procrastination and self-doubt is a common challenge faced by many individuals, particularly in the context of pursuing goals. The SMART goal-setting technique—Specific, Measurable, Achievable, Relevant, and Time-bound—provides a structured approach that can effectively combat these issues. By understanding the psychological mechanisms behind procrastination and self-doubt, as well as employing strategies rooted in the SMART framework, individuals can enhance their motivation, focus, and overall productivity.

Understanding Procrastination

Procrastination is often defined as the voluntary delay of an intended action despite expecting to be worse off for this delay (Steel, 2007). This behavior can stem from various psychological factors, including fear of failure, perfectionism, and low self-esteem. Research indicates that individuals who experience high levels of self-doubt are more prone to procrastination because they may feel overwhelmed by the pressure to perform perfectly (Sirois & Pychyl, 2013). This creates a vicious cycle: procrastination leads to increased anxiety and self-doubt, which in turn perpetuates further procrastination.

One effective way to combat procrastination is through the establishment of clear goals using the SMART framework. By setting specific and measurable objectives, individuals can break down overwhelming tasks into manageable steps. For example, rather than stating a vague goal such as "I want to study more," one could set a SMART goal: "I will study for two hours every weekday evening for the next month." This clarity helps reduce feelings of overwhelm and provides a clear path forward.

The Role of Self-Doubt

Self-doubt is another significant barrier that can hinder progress toward achieving goals. It often manifests as a lack of confidence in one's abilities or fear of negative evaluation by others. Research shows that self-doubt can lead to avoidance behaviors, including procrastination (Brunstein et al., 2010). When individuals doubt their capabilities, they may avoid taking action altogether or delay starting tasks until the last minute.

To address self-doubt effectively, it is essential to build a strong foundation of self-efficacy—the belief in one's ability to succeed. Bandura (1997) posits that self-efficacy influences the choices individuals make, their level of effort, and their persistence in the face of challenges. Setting SMART goals can enhance self-efficacy by providing clear benchmarks for success. As individuals achieve these goals, they reinforce their belief in their abilities and reduce feelings of self-doubt.

Utilizing SMART Goals to Overcome Procrastination

The SMART framework serves as an effective tool for overcoming procrastination by providing structure and clarity. Each component of SMART contributes uniquely to this process:

Specific: Specificity eliminates ambiguity and helps individuals understand precisely what they need to accomplish. By defining goals clearly—such as "I will complete my research paper by next Friday"—individuals can focus their efforts without getting lost in vague aspirations.

Measurable: Measurable goals allow individuals to track progress and celebrate small victories along the way. For example, breaking down a larger project into smaller tasks with measurable outcomes—such as "I will write 500 words each day"—creates tangible milestones that enhance motivation (Steel & Klingsieck, 2016).

Achievable: Setting achievable goals ensures that individuals do not become overwhelmed by unrealistic expectations. When goals are grounded in reality and aligned with one's current capabilities and resources, it becomes easier to take action. For instance, if someone struggles with time management due to work commitments, setting a goal like "I will study for 30 minutes each day" is more attainable than aiming for several hours.

Relevant: Relevant goals align with personal values and long-term aspirations. When individuals see how their goals connect to what truly matters to them—such as advancing in their careers or improving their health—they are more likely to stay motivated and committed (Ryan & Deci, 2000).

Time-bound: Time constraints create urgency and help prioritize tasks effectively. By establishing deadlines—like "I will submit my project by March 1st"—individuals are more likely to take consistent action rather than delaying until the last minute.

Personal Stories: Overcoming Procrastination and Self-Doubt

Casual anecdotes often illustrate how applying the SMART framework can help overcome procrastination and self-doubt effectively. Take the story of Alex, a college student who struggled with procrastination due to overwhelming coursework and fear of failure. Initially paralyzed by self-doubt, Alex decided to implement SMART goals into his study routine. He set specific objectives: "I will review lecture notes for one hour every day after class." By measuring his progress weekly and adjusting his study plan as needed, Alex gradually built confidence in his abilities. As he achieved these small goals consistently over time, his self-doubt diminished significantly.

Similarly, consider Maria's experience with her first job after college. Faced with new responsibilities and high expectations from her employer, she found herself procrastinating on important projects due to anxiety about her performance. To combat this issue, Maria turned to the SMART framework. She established specific deadlines for each project component: "I will complete the first draft of my report by Wednesday." By breaking down her tasks into manageable parts and setting realistic timelines, Maria not only overcame her tendency to procrastinate but also built her confidence in handling workplace challenges.

Strategies Beyond SMART Goals

While SMART goals are effective for combating procrastination and self-doubt, additional strategies can further enhance success. One such strategy involves creating accountability systems—Incorporating mindfulness practices can help individuals manage anxiety associated with self-doubt; mindfulness techniques have been shown to reduce stress levels and improve focus (Keng et al., 2011).

Moreover, recognizing underlying psychological barriers is crucial for addressing procrastination effectively. Individuals should take time to reflect on what drives their avoidance behaviors—whether it be fear of failure or perfectionism—and develop coping strategies accordingly (Steel & Klingsieck, 2016). Understanding these root causes allows individuals to tailor their approaches when setting goals.

Overcoming procrastination and self-doubt is essential for achieving personal and professional success. The SMART goal-setting technique provides a structured approach that enhances motivation while addressing these common barriers effectively. By setting Specific, Measurable, Achievable, Relevant, and Time-bound objectives, individuals can create clear pathways toward their aspirations while building confidence along the way. Through personal stories of triumph over procrastination and self-doubt combined with evidence-based strategies rooted in psychology, it becomes evident that anyone can overcome these challenges through intentional goal-setting practices.

Chapter 4

Breaking Down SMART Goals

Specific

Define a clear and precise goal

Measurable

Establish criteria to track progress

Achievable

Ensure the goal is attainable and realistic

Relevant

Align the goal with broader objectives

Time-bound

Set a deadline for goal completion

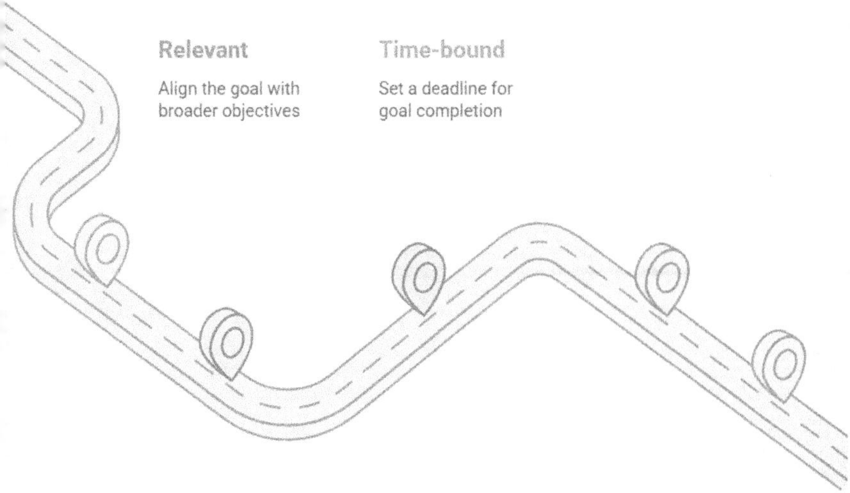

10. Specific: Defining goals clearly

The first component of the SMART goal-setting technique—Specific—plays a crucial role in ensuring that goals are clear, well-defined, and actionable. Goals that lack specificity can lead to confusion, lack of direction, and ultimately, failure to achieve desired outcomes. By articulating goals in precise terms, individuals and organizations can create a roadmap that guides their efforts and enhances their chances of success. This chapter will explore the importance of specificity in goal setting, supported by scientific research, historical context, and engaging anecdotes.

The Importance of Specificity

Specificity in goal setting refers to the clarity with which objectives are defined. A specific goal answers the fundamental questions of who, what, where, when, and why. For example, rather than stating a vague aspiration like "I want to get fit," a specific goal would be "I will join a gym and work out four days a week for at least 30 minutes each session." This level of detail removes ambiguity and provides a clear direction for action (Locke & Latham, 2002). Research has consistently shown that specific goals lead to higher performance compared to general or vague objectives. A meta-analysis conducted by Locke and Latham (2006) revealed that individuals who set specific goals were more likely to achieve them than those who set broad intentions.

The psychological basis for this phenomenon lies in the way our brains process information. When goals are specific, they activate relevant neural pathways associated with motivation and action. This activation enhances focus and directs attention toward tasks that contribute to achieving the goal (Schunk & Zimmerman, 2008). In contrast, vague goals can lead to cognitive overload and indecision, making it difficult for individuals to prioritize their efforts effectively.

Historical Context

The concept of specificity in goal setting is not new; it has been explored within various psychological theories over the years. Edwin Locke's Goal Setting Theory, developed in the late 1960s and early 1970s, emphasized the importance of setting clear and challenging goals as a means of enhancing performance (Locke & Latham, 2002). This theory laid the groundwork for understanding how specific goals can motivate individuals to exert greater effort and persist in the face of challenges.

Historically, organizations have recognized the value of specificity in goal setting as well. For instance, during the rise of management by objectives (MBO) in the 1980s, businesses began implementing structured goal-setting practices that emphasized clarity and accountability. MBO frameworks encouraged managers to set specific targets for their teams while aligning those objectives with broader organizational goals (Drucker, 1954). This approach not only improved productivity but also fostered a culture of transparency and collaboration within organizations.

Research Supporting Specificity

Numerous studies have demonstrated the effectiveness of specific goal setting across various contexts. For example, a study published in The Journal of Applied Psychology found that employees who set specific performance goals achieved significantly higher outcomes than those who set general goals (Locke & Latham, 2002). In an educational context, students who defined clear academic targets—such as "I will study for two hours every evening"—performed better than those with less defined aspirations (Schunk & Zimmerman, 2008).

Moreover, specificity is particularly beneficial when combined with other components of the SMART framework. For instance, when individuals set measurable and time-bound objectives alongside specific goals, they create a comprehensive plan that enhances motivation and accountability. A study by Pham and Taylor (1999) revealed that participants who engaged in both visualization and specific goal setting were more likely to pursue their objectives vigorously than those who did not employ these strategies.

Practical Applications: Crafting Specific Goals

To effectively implement specificity in goal setting, individuals should consider several key strategies:

1. Utilize the "Five W's": When defining goals, ask yourself who is involved (who), what you want to achieve (what), where it will take place (where), when you plan to accomplish it (when), and why it matters (why). This comprehensive approach ensures clarity from multiple perspectives.
2. Break Down Larger Goals: Large or long-term aspirations can often feel overwhelming. Breaking them down into smaller, specific milestones makes them more manageable and helps maintain motivation over time.
3. Write It Down: Documenting your specific goals increases commitment and serves as a constant reminder of your objectives. Research indicates that individuals who write down their goals are more likely to achieve them compared to those who do not (Matthews et al., 2020).
4. Review Regularly: Periodically reviewing your specific goals allows you to assess progress and make necessary adjustments. This ongoing reflection helps maintain focus on what truly matters while ensuring that your objectives remain relevant.
5. Seek Feedback: Sharing your specific goals with trusted friends or colleagues can provide valuable insights and support as you work toward achievement.

Defining goals clearly through specificity is essential for effective goal setting within the SMART framework. Specificity enhances motivation by providing clarity and direction while activating neural pathways associated with action-oriented behavior. Supported by historical context and extensive research findings, it is evident that specific goals lead to higher performance across various domains.

By incorporating personal stories that illustrate the power of specificity alongside practical strategies for crafting clear objectives, individuals can harness this component of SMART goal setting effectively. As they embark on their journeys toward achieving their aspirations—whether personal or professional—they will find that specificity serves as a guiding light on their path to success.

11. Measurable: Setting quantifiable milestones

The second component of the SMART goal-setting technique, Measurable, emphasizes the importance of establishing quantifiable milestones that allow individuals to track their progress toward achieving their goals. This aspect is crucial because it provides a clear framework for assessing whether one is on track to meet their objectives. By incorporating measurable criteria, individuals can maintain motivation, make necessary adjustments, and ultimately enhance their chances of success. This chapter will delve into the significance of measurability in goal setting, supported by scientific research, historical context, and engaging anecdotes.

The Importance of Measurability

Measurability in goal setting refers to the ability to quantify progress toward achieving a specific objective. When goals are measurable, individuals can track their advancement and evaluate their performance against established benchmarks. For example, instead of setting a vague goal such as "I want to improve my fitness," a measurable goal would be "I will lose five pounds in two months by exercising three times a week and eating healthier." This clarity not only provides a tangible target but also allows for ongoing assessment of progress (Locke & Latham, 2002).

Research has shown that measurable goals significantly enhance motivation and performance. A study published in The Journal of Applied Psychology found that employees who set measurable performance goals achieved significantly higher outcomes than those who set general or non-quantifiable goals (Locke & Latham, 2006). The psychological basis for this phenomenon lies in the feedback loop created by measurable milestones; as individuals achieve these milestones, they experience a sense of accomplishment that reinforces their motivation to continue working toward their ultimate objectives.

Historical Context

The concept of measurability in goal setting has been recognized for decades, particularly within the field of management and organizational behavior. The rise of management by objectives (MBO) in the 1950s and 1960s emphasized the importance of setting clear, quantifiable targets for employees (Drucker, 1954). MBO frameworks encouraged managers to establish specific performance indicators that could be measured over time. This structured approach not only improved productivity but also fostered a culture of accountability within organizations.

Moreover, the development of performance metrics in various industries has further highlighted the significance of measurability in goal setting. For instance, in sales and marketing, organizations often establish key performance indicators (KPIs) to assess progress toward revenue targets or customer acquisition goals. These metrics provide valuable insights into performance trends and help identify areas for improvement.

Research Supporting Measurability

Numerous studies have demonstrated the effectiveness of measurable goal setting across various contexts. For example, a meta-analysis conducted by Locke and Latham (2006) revealed that specific and measurable goals lead to higher performance compared to vague or easily achievable objectives. In an educational context, students who defined clear academic targets—such as "I will study for two hours every evening"—performed better than those with less defined aspirations (Schunk & Zimmerman, 2008).

Additionally, research has shown that providing regular feedback on progress enhances motivation and commitment when pursuing measurable goals. A study by Harkin et al. (2016) found that individuals who received feedback on their progress toward specific goals were more likely to persist in their efforts and achieve desired outcomes than those who did not receive such feedback.

Casual Stories: The Power of Measurable Goals

Personal anecdotes often illustrate how setting measurable milestones can lead to successful outcomes. Consider the story of Mark, an aspiring marathon runner who struggled with maintaining motivation during his training. Initially, he set a vague goal: "I want to run a marathon." However, after learning about the SMART framework, Mark transformed his goal into something measurable: "I will complete a marathon in under four hours within six months." To achieve this objective, he broke down his training into quantifiable milestones: "I will run three times a week and gradually increase my long run by one mile each week."

By tracking his progress through a running app that recorded his distances and times, Mark remained motivated as he celebrated each milestone achieved along the way. As he saw his times improve and his endurance increase, his confidence grew significantly. Ultimately, Mark completed his marathon in three hours and fifty-five minutes—a testament to the power of setting measurable goals.

Practical Applications: Crafting Measurable Goals

To effectively implement measurability in goal setting, individuals should consider several key strategies:

1. Define Clear Metrics: When establishing goals, determine how success will be measured. This could involve quantifying

outcomes such as sales figures, weight loss amounts, or project completion rates.

2. Set Milestones: Break down larger goals into smaller milestones that can be tracked over time. For example, if your goal is to increase sales revenue by 20% over six months, establish monthly targets that contribute to this overall objective.
3. Utilize Tracking Tools: Use tools such as spreadsheets or mobile apps to monitor progress regularly. Visual representations of data can enhance motivation by providing tangible evidence of advancement.
4. Review Progress Regularly: Schedule regular check-ins to assess progress toward measurable goals. This reflection allows for adjustments if necessary and reinforces commitment to achieving objectives.
5. Celebrate Achievements: Recognize and celebrate milestones achieved along the way. Acknowledging progress fosters positive reinforcement and encourages continued effort toward larger goals.

Setting quantifiable milestones through measurability is essential for effective goal setting within the SMART framework. Measurable goals enhance motivation by providing clarity and direction while activating neural pathways associated with action-oriented behavior. Supported by historical context and extensive research findings, it is evident that measurable objectives lead to higher performance across various domains.

By incorporating personal stories that illustrate the power of measurability alongside practical strategies for crafting clear metrics, individuals can harness this component of SMART goal setting effectively. As they embark on their journeys toward achieving their aspirations—whether personal or professional—they will find that measurability serves as an essential tool on their path to success.

12. Achievable: Ensuring goals are realistic

The third component of the SMART goal-setting technique—Achievable—is vital for ensuring that the goals set are not only ambitious but also realistic and attainable. This aspect of goal setting emphasizes the importance of aligning objectives with an individual's capabilities, resources, and circumstances. By establishing achievable goals, individuals can foster motivation, commitment, and a sense of accomplishment, ultimately leading to successful outcomes. This chapter will explore the significance of achievability in goal setting, supported by scientific research, historical context, and engaging anecdotes.

The Importance of Achievability

Achievability in goal setting refers to the extent to which a goal can realistically be accomplished given the available resources, skills, and time constraints. Setting goals that are too ambitious or unrealistic can lead to frustration, decreased motivation, and ultimately failure (Locke & Latham, 2002). Conversely, goals that are perceived as achievable can enhance self-efficacy—the belief in one's ability to succeed—which is a critical factor in motivating individuals to pursue their objectives (Bandura, 1997).

Research has shown that individuals are more likely to commit to and achieve goals that they believe are attainable. A study conducted by Schunk (2003) found that students who set achievable academic goals demonstrated higher levels of motivation and persistence compared to those who set overly ambitious targets. This finding underscores the importance of ensuring that goals are challenging enough to promote growth while remaining within reach.

Historical Context

The concept of achievability in goal setting has been explored within various psychological theories over the years. Edwin Locke's Goal Setting Theory, developed in the late 1960s and early 1970s, emphasizes the importance of setting specific and challenging goals while also recognizing the need for those goals to be attainable (Locke & Latham, 2002). This theory laid the groundwork for understanding how achievable goals can motivate individuals to exert greater effort and persist in the face of challenges.

Historically, organizations have recognized the significance of achievability in goal setting as well. The rise of management by objectives (MBO) in the 1950s emphasized the importance of aligning individual performance targets with organizational capabilities and resources (Drucker, 1954). MBO frameworks encouraged managers to establish realistic performance indicators that could be achieved within a specified timeframe. This structured approach not only improved productivity but also fostered a culture of accountability and support within organizations.

Research Supporting Achievability

Numerous studies have demonstrated the effectiveness of achievable goal setting across various contexts. For example, a meta-analysis conducted by Locke and Latham (2006) revealed that specific and achievable goals lead to higher performance compared to vague or overly ambitious objectives. In an educational context, students who defined clear academic targets—such as "I will study for two hours every evening"—performed better than those with less defined aspirations (Schunk & Zimmerman, 2008).

Moreover, research has shown that providing individuals with resources and support can enhance their perception of achievability. A study by Bandura et al. (2003) found that individuals who received guidance and encouragement from mentors were more likely to set achievable goals and persist in their efforts compared to those who did not receive such support. This highlights the importance of fostering an environment that promotes realistic goal setting through adequate resources and encouragement.

Casual Stories: The Power of Achievable Goals

Personal anecdotes often illustrate how setting achievable milestones can lead to successful outcomes. Consider the story of Rachel, an aspiring entrepreneur who dreamed of launching her own bakery. Initially overwhelmed by her ambition, she set a vague goal: "I want to open my bakery." However, after learning about the SMART framework, Rachel transformed her goal into something more achievable: "I will start my bakery business by first selling baked goods at local farmers' markets over the next six months."

By breaking down her larger aspiration into smaller, attainable steps—such as researching recipes, obtaining necessary permits, and creating a marketing plan—Rachel found herself more motivated to take action. As she successfully sold her goods at markets each week, she gained valuable experience and confidence in her abilities. Ultimately, Rachel's bakery became a reality because she established achievable milestones along her journey.

Similarly, consider Mark's experience with fitness. Initially frustrated by his lack of progress toward weight loss goals, he decided to implement achievable targets into his routine. Instead of aiming for an unrealistic goal like "I want to lose 30 pounds in one month," Mark set a more realistic objective: "I will lose one pound per week by exercising three times a week and tracking my food intake." By focusing on this attainable target, Mark was able to celebrate small victories each week as he reached his weight loss milestones. This sense of achievement kept him motivated throughout his fitness journey.

Practical Applications: Crafting Achievable Goals

To effectively implement achievability in goal setting, individuals should consider several key strategies:

1. Assess Resources: Before setting a goal, evaluate available resources such as time, skills, finances, and support systems. This assessment helps ensure that your objectives align with what you can realistically achieve.
2. Set Incremental Milestones: Break larger goals into smaller milestones that can be achieved gradually over time. For instance, if your ultimate objective is to run a marathon within six months, start with achievable targets like completing a 5K or half-marathon first.
3. Consider Past Experiences: Reflect on previous successes or challenges when setting new goals. Understanding what worked well or what obstacles you faced can inform your approach to establishing achievable objectives.
4. Seek Feedback: Share your goals with trusted friends or mentors who can provide constructive feedback on their achievability. External perspectives can help identify potential pitfalls or areas for improvement.
5. Be Flexible: Recognize that circumstances may change over time; be willing to adjust your goals as needed based on new information or changing situations.

Ensuring that goals are realistic through achievability is essential for effective goal setting within the SMART framework. Achievable goals enhance motivation by providing clarity while fostering self-efficacy—the belief in one's ability to succeed. Supported by historical context and extensive research findings, it is evident that achievable objectives lead to higher performance across various domains.

By incorporating personal stories that illustrate the power of achievability alongside practical strategies for crafting realistic milestones, individuals can harness this component of SMART goal setting effectively. As they embark on their journeys toward achieving their aspirations—whether personal or professional—they will find that making their goals achievable serves as a crucial stepping stone on their path to success.

13. Relevant: Aligning goals with personal or organizational objectives

The fourth component of the SMART goal-setting technique—Relevant—is essential for ensuring that the goals set are meaningful and aligned with broader personal or organizational objectives. Goals that are relevant resonate with an individual's values, aspirations, and the overarching mission of an organization. By establishing relevance in goal setting, individuals and teams can enhance motivation, commitment, and ultimately achieve successful outcomes. This chapter will explore the significance of relevance in goal setting, supported by scientific research, historical context, and engaging anecdotes.

The Importance of Relevance

Relevance in goal setting refers to the degree to which a goal aligns with an individual's or organization's long-term objectives and values. When goals are relevant, they contribute meaningfully to broader ambitions and provide a sense of purpose (AchieveIt, 2024). For example, if an employee's goal is to improve customer service skills, this objective should align with the organization's mission to deliver exceptional customer experiences. This alignment fosters a sense of ownership and commitment to achieving the goal.

Research has demonstrated that relevant goals significantly enhance motivation and performance. A study by Locke and Latham (2006) found that when individuals perceive their goals as aligned with their personal values or organizational missions, they are more likely to exert greater effort and persist in their endeavors. This sense of alignment not only reinforces motivation but also enhances job satisfaction and overall well-being.

Historical Context

The concept of relevance in goal setting has been recognized for decades within various psychological theories and management practices. The development of Management by Objectives (MBO) in the mid-20th century emphasized the importance of aligning individual performance targets with organizational goals (Drucker, 1954). MBO frameworks encouraged managers to establish specific objectives that contributed directly to the company's mission, thereby fostering a culture of accountability and collaboration.

Furthermore, the rise of strategic planning in organizations during the 1980s highlighted the significance of aligning operational goals with long-term strategic objectives. Organizations began to recognize that for goals to be effective, they must not only be specific and measurable but also relevant to the overall direction of the organization. This shift in thinking laid the groundwork for contemporary approaches to goal setting that prioritize alignment with broader objectives.

Research Supporting Relevance

Numerous studies have demonstrated the effectiveness of relevant goal setting across various contexts. For instance, a study conducted by Harkin et al. (2016) revealed that individuals who set goals aligned with their values experienced higher levels of motivation and commitment compared to those who pursued unrelated objectives. In an educational context, students who defined clear academic targets that resonated with their personal aspirations performed better than those with less relevant goals (Schunk & Zimmerman, 2008).

Additionally, research has shown that organizations that prioritize relevance in goal setting experience improved performance outcomes. A study by Kaplan and Norton (1996) introduced the Balanced Scorecard approach, which emphasizes aligning organizational objectives with strategic priorities. This framework has been widely adopted by organizations seeking to enhance performance through relevant goal setting.

Casual Stories: The Power of Relevant Goals

Personal anecdotes often illustrate how establishing relevant goals can lead to successful outcomes. Consider the story of Jessica, a marketing professional who felt unfulfilled in her role due to a lack of alignment between her personal values and her job responsibilities. After reflecting on her aspirations, she decided to pursue a relevant goal: "I will develop a marketing campaign that promotes sustainable products for our company." By aligning her work with her passion for sustainability, Jessica found renewed motivation and creativity in her efforts.

As she crafted her campaign, Jessica involved her team in brainstorming sessions focused on eco-friendly messaging and community engagement strategies. The result was not only a successful marketing campaign but also increased employee morale as team members felt connected to a cause they believed in. This experience highlights how relevant goals can foster collaboration and drive positive outcomes within organizations.

Similarly, consider Tom's experience as a sales manager at a technology company. Initially focused solely on increasing sales numbers without considering alignment with customer needs or company values, Tom realized he needed to redefine his approach. He set a new relevant goal: "I will train my sales team on consultative selling techniques that prioritize understanding customer needs." By aligning his team's efforts with the organization's mission to provide value-driven solutions, Tom not only improved sales performance but also enhanced customer satisfaction.

Practical Applications: Crafting Relevant Goals

To effectively implement relevance in goal setting, individuals should consider several key strategies:

1. Understand Organizational Values: Familiarize yourself with your organization's mission statement, core values, and strategic priorities. This understanding will help you identify areas where your goals can contribute meaningfully.
2. Align Personal Aspirations: Reflect on your personal values and long-term career aspirations when setting goals. Ensure that your objectives resonate with what truly matters to you; this alignment fosters intrinsic motivation.
3. Engage Stakeholders: Involve colleagues or team members in discussions about goal alignment. Collaborative dialogue can uncover insights into how individual goals can support broader organizational objectives.
4. Review Regularly: Periodically assess your goals to ensure they remain relevant as circumstances change. Flexibility is key; be willing to adjust your objectives based on new information or evolving priorities.
5. Celebrate Contributions: Acknowledge how achieving relevant goals contributes to both personal satisfaction and organizational success. Recognizing these connections reinforces commitment and motivation.

Aligning goals with personal or organizational objectives through relevance is essential for effective goal setting within the SMART framework. Relevant goals enhance motivation by providing clarity and purpose while fostering a sense of ownership over one's objectives. Supported by historical context and extensive research findings, it is evident that relevant objectives lead to higher performance across various domains.

14. Time-bound: Setting deadlines for accountability

The final component of the SMART goal-setting technique—Time-bound—is essential for establishing a clear timeline within which goals are to be achieved. Setting deadlines not only creates a sense of urgency but also enhances accountability, ensuring that individuals stay focused and committed to their objectives. This chapter will explore the significance of time-bound goals, supported by scientific research, historical context, and engaging anecdotes.

The Importance of Time-Bound Goals

Time-bound goals are characterized by specific deadlines that define when an objective should be completed. This aspect of goal setting is crucial for several reasons. First, deadlines create a sense of urgency that motivates individuals to take action. When people know they have a limited timeframe to achieve their goals, they are more likely to prioritize tasks and avoid procrastination (Harkin et al., 2016). For example, instead of saying, "I want to lose weight," a time-bound goal would specify, "I will lose 10 pounds in three months." This clarity not only helps individuals stay focused but also encourages them to break down their larger objectives into manageable tasks with specific timelines.

Research has shown that time constraints enhance performance by fostering accountability. A study published in Psychological Science found that individuals who set deadlines for their goals were more likely to achieve them than those without time constraints (Ariely & Wertenbroch, 2002). The pressure of an impending deadline can drive individuals to take consistent action and maintain momentum toward their objectives.

Historical Context

The concept of time-bound goal setting has been recognized for decades within various psychological theories and management practices. The development of Management by Objectives (MBO) in the mid-20th century emphasized the importance of establishing clear timelines for achieving performance targets (Drucker, 1954). MBO frameworks encouraged managers to set specific deadlines for employee objectives, thereby fostering a culture of accountability and performance measurement.

Moreover, the rise of project management methodologies in the late 20th century highlighted the significance of time-bound goals in achieving successful outcomes. Techniques such as Gantt charts and critical path analysis emphasize the importance of defining timelines for project milestones and deliverables. These structured approaches have been widely adopted across industries, reinforcing the notion that time constraints are integral to effective goal setting.

Research Supporting Time-Bound Goals

Numerous studies have demonstrated the effectiveness of time-bound goal setting across various contexts. For instance, a meta-analysis conducted by Locke and Latham (2006) revealed that specific and time-constrained goals lead to higher performance compared to vague or open-ended objectives. In an educational context, students who defined clear deadlines for their assignments performed better than those without specified due dates (Schunk & Zimmerman, 2008).

Additionally, research has shown that providing regular feedback on progress toward time-bound goals enhances motivation and commitment. A study by Harkin et al. (2016) found that individuals who received feedback on their progress relative to established deadlines were more likely to persist in their efforts and achieve desired outcomes than those who did not receive such feedback.

Casual Stories: The Impact of Time-Bound Goals

Personal anecdotes often illustrate how establishing time-bound goals can lead to successful outcomes. Consider the story of Alex, a graduate student who struggled with completing his thesis due to procrastination and lack of structure. Initially overwhelmed by the enormity of his project, he decided to implement SMART goals into his writing process. Alex set a specific deadline: "I will complete my thesis draft by May 1st." To ensure he stayed on track, he broke this larger goal into smaller milestones with corresponding deadlines: "I will write one chapter every two weeks."

As the deadline approached, Alex felt a renewed sense of urgency that motivated him to write consistently. By tracking his progress against these milestones and holding himself accountable for meeting each deadline, he successfully completed his thesis on time. This experience underscores how time-bound goals can create a structured environment conducive to productivity.

Similarly, consider Sarah's experience with her fitness journey. Initially uncertain about how to achieve her weight loss goals, she decided to set a clear deadline: "I will lose 15 pounds in three months." To make this goal manageable, Sarah developed a workout schedule with specific sessions planned each week and tracked her progress through regular weigh-ins.

As she approached her deadline, Sarah found herself motivated by the impending target date; she was more disciplined about her workouts and meal planning. The clear timeline allowed her to celebrate small victories along the way—such as losing five pounds in the first month—which reinforced her commitment to achieving her ultimate goal.

Practical Applications: Crafting Time-Bound Goals

To effectively implement time constraints in goal setting, individuals should consider several key strategies:

1. Define Clear Deadlines: When establishing goals, determine specific dates or timeframes by which you aim to achieve your objectives. This clarity provides a target to work toward and helps maintain focus.
2. Break It Down: For larger or long-term goals, break them down into smaller milestones with their own deadlines. This makes the overall objective more manageable and allows for progress evaluation along the way.
3. Create a Sense of Urgency: Use deadlines to instill a sense of urgency in your efforts. A clear timeline encourages action and helps prioritize tasks effectively.
4. Be Realistic: Ensure that your deadlines are realistic and achievable within the given timeframe. Consider potential obstacles or constraints that may impact your ability to meet your targets.
5. Review Progress Regularly: Schedule regular check-ins to assess your progress toward time-bound goals. This reflection allows you to make adjustments if necessary while reinforcing commitment.

Setting deadlines through time-bound goals is essential for effective goal setting within the SMART framework. Time constraints enhance motivation by creating urgency while fostering accountability in pursuing objectives. Supported by historical context and extensive research findings, it is evident that time-bound objectives lead to higher performance across various domains.

Workout Your Plan of Action

List of your SMART Goals

Chapter 5

Pareto Principle

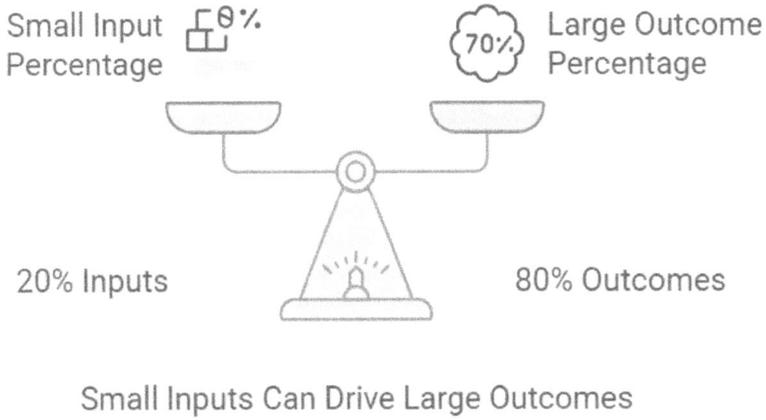

15. 80/20 Pareto Principle

The 80/20 Pareto Principle, also known simply as the Pareto Principle, is a widely recognized concept that posits that a small percentage of causes often leads to a large percentage of effects. Specifically, it suggests that approximately 80% of outcomes result from 20% of inputs. This principle was first introduced by the Italian economist Vilfredo Pareto in 1906 when he observed that about 80% of the land in Italy was owned by just 20% of the population. His findings highlighted an unequal distribution of resources, which he theorized could be applicable in various contexts beyond wealth distribution.

Over time, the Pareto Principle has been adapted and applied across multiple fields, particularly in business, economics, and quality control. In the 1940s, management consultant Dr. Joseph Juran expanded upon Pareto's work by applying the principle to quality management. He emphasized the importance of identifying the "vital few" factors that significantly impact results compared to the "trivial many." This focus on prioritization allows organizations to allocate resources more effectively, enhancing productivity and efficiency (TechTarget).

Applications of the Pareto Principle

The 80/20 rule has numerous practical applications:

Business Management: In a business context, it is often cited that 80% of sales come from 20% of clients. This insight encourages companies to focus their marketing and customer service efforts on their most valuable customers (Investopedia)

Time Management: Individuals can apply the principle to their personal productivity by identifying which tasks yield the most significant results. For example, it may be discovered that 20% of daily activities contribute to 80% of overall productivity (Indeed).

Quality Control: In quality management, it is common for a small number of defects or issues to account for the majority of problems within a product or service. By addressing these critical few issues, organizations can significantly improve quality and reduce costs.

Software Development: The principle also applies in software engineering, where it is often found that 20% of bugs cause 80% of system failures. By prioritizing fixes for these critical bugs, developers can enhance system reliability more efficiently (TechTarget)

Pareto Principle in Goal Setting

The Pareto Principle, commonly referred to as the 80/20 rule, is a crucial concept in effective goal setting. It asserts that approximately 80% of outcomes stem from just 20% of inputs or efforts. This principle can significantly enhance how individuals and organizations prioritize their goals, ensuring that they focus on the most impactful actions. When aligned with the SMART framework—Specific, Measurable, Achievable, Relevant, and Time-bound—the Pareto Principle becomes an even more powerful tool for achieving success.

Importance of the Pareto Principle in Goal Setting

Focus on High-Impact Activities: The essence of the 80/20 rule is identifying which tasks yield the most significant results. By recognizing that a small fraction of activities can lead to substantial outcomes, individuals can concentrate their efforts on these high-impact tasks. For instance, if a person has ten goals, applying the Pareto Principle allows them to identify which two goals will contribute most to their overall success. This prioritization helps avoid wasting time on less productive activities that contribute minimally to desired results.

Enhanced Efficiency: By focusing on the vital few tasks that drive results, individuals can work more efficiently. The Pareto Principle encourages a mindset where one seeks to do less but achieve more. This approach not only reduces overwhelm but also leads to better time management and productivity. For example, a salesperson might discover that 20% of their clients generate 80% of their sales; thus, they can allocate more time and resources to nurturing those key relationships.

Clarity in Decision-Making: The 80/20 rule simplifies decision-making by helping individuals discern which goals are worth pursuing based on their potential impact. This clarity enables more strategic planning and resource allocation, ensuring that efforts align with high-priority objectives.

16. Identifying the Critical 20%

Techniques for Identifying High-Impact Tasks or Activities

To effectively apply the 80/20 Rule, it is crucial to identify which tasks or activities constitute the critical 20% that will drive the majority of your results. Here are some techniques to achieve this:

Data Analysis: Review past performance data to identify patterns. For instance, if you are in sales, analyze which clients or products have generated the most revenue. This quantitative approach helps pinpoint where your efforts have historically yielded the highest returns.

Feedback and Reflection: Regularly seek feedback from peers, mentors, or supervisors about which of your activities they perceive as most impactful. Reflecting on your own experiences can also help you recognize which tasks have led to significant achievements in the past.

Activity Logging: Keep a detailed log of your daily activities for a week or two. Afterward, categorize these activities based on their outcomes. This practice allows you to visualize where you spend your time and which activities correlate with meaningful results.

Goal Alignment: Ensure that the tasks you identify align with your overarching goals. This alignment guarantees that your focus remains on activities that contribute directly to your desired outcomes.

Distinguishing Between Productive and Unproductive Efforts

Identifying productive versus unproductive efforts is essential for maximizing efficiency:

Outcome-Oriented Evaluation: Assess each task based on its outcomes rather than its effort. A task may require significant time but yield minimal results; conversely, a small task may lead to substantial benefits.

Use of Metrics: Establish clear metrics for evaluating productivity. For example, if your goal is to increase website traffic, track metrics like unique visitors generated by specific marketing campaigns to determine which efforts are most effective.

Time Analysis: Consider how much time you spend on various tasks versus the results achieved. Tasks that consume excessive time with little payoff should be re-evaluated.

Prioritization Strategies

Once you have identified the critical 20%, it's essential to prioritize these tasks effectively:

Focusing Energy and Resources on Key Tasks That Drive the Most Results

1. Eisenhower Matrix: Use this decision-making tool to categorize tasks into four quadrants based on urgency and importance:
    a. Urgent and Important: Do these tasks immediately.
    b. Important but Not Urgent: Schedule these tasks.
    c. Urgent but Not Important: Delegate these tasks if possible.
    d. Not Urgent and Not Important: Eliminate these tasks.

2. ABC Prioritization Method: Assign an "A," "B," or "C" label to each task based on its importance:
    A (High Priority): Must be done today.
    B (Medium Priority): Should be done soon.
    C (Low Priority): Nice to do but not essential.

3. Time Blocking: Allocate specific blocks of time in your calendar dedicated solely to high-priority tasks. This method prevents distractions and ensures focused work on what matters most.

Time Management Techniques Inspired by the Pareto Principle

Pomodoro Technique: Work in focused bursts (typically 25 minutes) followed by short breaks (5 minutes). This technique helps maintain concentration on high-impact tasks while preventing burnout.

Batch Processing: Group similar tasks together and complete them in one go rather than switching between different types of work. This minimizes context-switching costs and enhances efficiency.

Set Clear Deadlines: Establish deadlines for high-priority tasks to create a sense of urgency and accountability, ensuring they receive the attention they deserve.

Eliminating or Delegating the Non-Essential 80%

To maximize effectiveness, it is vital to minimize distractions and low-value activities:

Strategies to Minimize Distractions and Low-Value Activities

Identify Time Wasters: Conduct an audit of your daily routines to identify activities that consume time without contributing meaningfully to your goals—such as excessive social media use or unnecessary meetings.
Establish Boundaries: Set clear boundaries regarding availability for meetings or interruptions during focused work periods.

Communicate these boundaries with colleagues or family members.

Use Technology Wisely: Leverage tools like website blockers or productivity apps that help limit distractions during work hours, allowing you to concentrate on high-impact activities.

Regular Reviews: Periodically review your goals and activities to ensure alignment with your priorities and adjust as necessary to eliminate any non-essential commitments.

Delegation Techniques for Tasks That Don't Directly Contribute to Your Goals

Assess Delegation Opportunities: Identify tasks that can be delegated without compromising quality or outcomes—these often include administrative duties or routine processes that do not require your direct involvement.

Empower Team Members: If you lead a team, empower members by entrusting them with responsibilities aligned with their strengths and skills. This fosters a sense of ownership while freeing up your time for more critical tasks.

Use Project Management Tools: Implement project management software (such as Trello or Asana) that facilitates task assignment and tracking, making delegation more manageable and transparent.

Provide Clear Instructions: When delegating tasks, ensure you provide clear instructions and expectations so that team members understand their responsibilities and can execute them effectively.

Applying the 80/20 Rule to goal setting involves identifying high-impact tasks, prioritizing them effectively, and minimizing distractions through elimination or delegation of non-essential activities. By focusing energy on the critical few efforts that drive significant results, individuals can enhance their productivity and achieve their goals more efficiently. Integrating these strategies into daily practices empowers individuals to work smarter rather than harder, ultimately leading to greater success in both personal and professional endeavors.

Chapter 6

Parkinson's Law

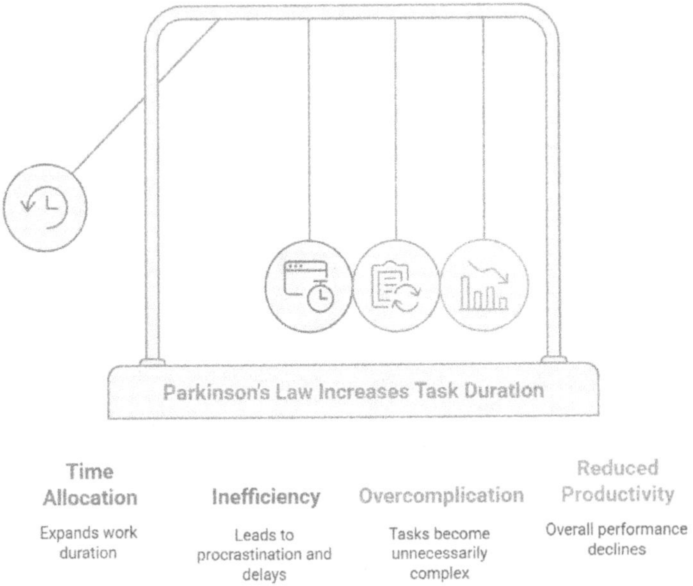

17. Parkinson's Law

Parkinson's Law is succinctly defined as "work expands to fill the time available for its completion." This principle suggests that the amount of work required to complete a task will increase to match the time allotted for it, regardless of the actual complexity or necessity of the task.

The term was coined by Cyril Northcote Parkinson, a British naval historian, in a humorous essay published in The Economist in 1955. In this essay, Parkinson illustrated his point with a whimsical example of a woman whose sole task for the day was to send a postcard. Despite the task only requiring a few minutes, she managed to occupy her entire day with various distractions and deliberations, demonstrating how tasks can expand to fill available time. Parkinson’s observations were not limited to individual productivity; he also noted that bureaucratic organizations tend to grow in size and complexity, often without corresponding increases in workload (Parkinson, 1955).

Parkinson's Law has since been recognized as a critical concept in time management and productivity, emphasizing the importance of setting realistic deadlines and prioritizing tasks effectively. It highlights how excessive time allowances can lead to inefficiencies, as individuals may procrastinate or overcomplicate tasks when they feel they have ample time to complete them (Growth Method).

In contemporary settings, understanding Parkinson's Law can help individuals and organizations streamline their processes, eliminate unnecessary delays, and improve overall performance by encouraging more focused work habits.

The impact of Parkinson's Law on productivity and goal achievement is significant, as it highlights how the perception of time can influence work behavior. Understanding this principle is crucial for setting SMART (Specific, Measurable, Achievable, Relevant, Time-bound) goals, as it underscores the importance of time constraints and prioritization in achieving desired outcomes.

The Impact of Parkinson's Law on Productivity and Goal Achievement

Parkinson's Law asserts that "work expands to fill the time available for its completion," which can lead to inefficiencies and procrastination. When individuals are given an extended period to complete a task, they may take longer than necessary due to several factors:

Procrastination: The absence of a pressing deadline often results in delays, as individuals may postpone starting tasks until the last minute. This behavior can lead to rushed work and increased stress, ultimately compromising the quality of the output.

Scope Creep: With more time available, there is a tendency for tasks to become overly complicated or to include unnecessary details. This phenomenon can dilute focus and lead to outcomes that do not align with original objectives.

Resource Mismanagement: Extended timelines can result in inefficient use of resources, both human and financial. When tasks are allowed to expand indefinitely, teams may misallocate their time and effort, impacting overall productivity.

Reduced Motivation: A lack of urgency can diminish motivation among team members. When deadlines are not clearly defined, there is less incentive to complete tasks promptly, leading to a culture of complacency.

18. The Relationship Between Deadlines and Task Complexity

Deadlines play a crucial role in shaping how tasks are approached and completed. The relationship between deadlines and task complexity can significantly influence productivity and efficiency. Generally, simpler tasks tend to be more responsive to deadlines, while complex tasks may not benefit from arbitrary time constraints in the same way.

How Deadlines Affect Task Complexity

Increased Focus: For low-complexity tasks, deadlines create a sense of urgency that can enhance focus and drive completion. When individuals know they have a limited time to finish a straightforward task, they are more likely to concentrate their efforts and avoid distractions, leading to higher efficiency.

Cognitive Load: Conversely, high-complexity tasks often involve numerous components and interdependencies. In these scenarios, strict deadlines may induce stress rather than motivation. The cognitive load associated with complex tasks can overwhelm individuals when they feel pressured to meet an impending deadline, potentially leading to decreased performance and quality of work (ResearchGate) .

Procrastination: The tendency to procrastinate can also be influenced by task complexity. Individuals may delay starting complex projects until closer to the deadline, believing they can manage the workload in a shorter time frame. This behavior often leads to rushed work and subpar outcomes, particularly when the complexity of the task requires more thoughtful consideration and planning (Indeed) .

Examples of How Unnecessarily Long Timeframes Reduce Efficiency

Scope Creep: When deadlines are set too far in the future, there is a risk of scope creep—where the project expands beyond its original objectives due to a lack of urgency. For instance, if a team is given six months to complete a project that could realistically be finished in three months, they may introduce unnecessary features or changes that complicate the project without adding significant value (Monitask).

Diluted Focus: Extended timeframes can lead to diluted focus on the task at hand. For example, if employees are given a month to complete a report, they may spend excessive time on research or revisions that could have been streamlined with a tighter deadline. This not only wastes time but can also lead to diminishing returns as the quality of work does not necessarily improve with additional time (Indeed).

Reduced Accountability: Long deadlines can diminish accountability among team members. When individuals know they have ample time, they may not feel compelled to take ownership of their responsibilities, leading to delays and inefficiencies in collaborative environments (Monitask).

Increased Stress Leading Up to Deadlines: Ironically, while long deadlines might seem beneficial for reducing stress by providing ample time, they can create anxiety as individuals approach the end of an extended timeframe without having made significant progress. This last-minute rush can lead to mistakes and oversights that compromise quality (Indeed).

19. Using Parkinson's Law to Enhance SMART Goals

Setting Time-Bound Goals

The Importance of Realistic Yet Challenging Deadlines

Setting deadlines is crucial for effective goal achievement. Realistic yet challenging deadlines create a sense of urgency that encourages individuals to focus their efforts and avoid procrastination. When deadlines are too lenient, they can lead to inefficiencies and wasted opportunities, as individuals may not feel compelled to take immediate action. Conversely, overly aggressive deadlines can induce stress and anxiety, negatively impacting performance.

To strike the right balance, it is essential to establish deadlines that are achievable while still pushing individuals to perform at their best. Research indicates that setting shorter deadlines can lead to increased productivity by forcing individuals to concentrate on high-priority tasks and eliminate distractions.

How to Define "Time-Bound" Effectively Within SMART Goals

In the context of SMART goals, "time-bound" refers to the establishment of clear deadlines for when a goal should be achieved. Here are some strategies for defining time-bound elements effectively:

1. Be Specific: Instead of vague timelines like "soon" or "later," use precise dates or timeframes. For example, "Complete the project by March 15" is more effective than "Complete the project soon."

2. Incorporate Milestones: Break larger goals into smaller milestones with their own deadlines. This approach not only makes the overall goal more manageable but also provides opportunities for regular progress checks.

3. Set Self-Imposed Deadlines: In addition to external deadlines, consider establishing personal deadlines that are earlier than necessary. This practice helps create a buffer for unexpected challenges while maintaining a sense of urgency (Asana) .

4. Review and Adjust: Regularly assess progress toward your goals and be willing to adjust timelines as needed based on changing circumstances or new information.

By effectively defining the time-bound aspect of SMART goals, individuals can harness the power of Parkinson's Law to enhance focus and productivity.

Breaking Goals into Smaller Tasks

Creating Mini-Deadlines to Avoid Over-Expansion of Tasks

One effective strategy for combating Parkinson's Law is breaking larger goals into smaller, actionable tasks with specific mini-deadlines. This approach prevents tasks from expanding unnecessarily and helps maintain momentum throughout the project lifecycle.

1. Task Decomposition: Start by identifying all the components required to achieve a larger goal. For instance, if your goal is to launch a new marketing campaign, break it down into smaller tasks such as market research, content creation, design development, and campaign execution.

2. Set Mini-Deadlines: Assign specific deadlines for each smaller task. For example, you might set a deadline of one week for completing market research and two weeks for content creation. These mini-deadlines help keep progress on track while preventing procrastination (Fellow).

3. Regular Check-Ins: Schedule regular check-ins to assess progress on these smaller tasks. This practice ensures accountability and allows for adjustments if any tasks are falling behind schedule.

Ensuring Specific and Measurable Milestones

When breaking down goals into smaller tasks, it's essential to ensure that each task is specific and measurable:

- Specificity: Clearly define what needs to be accomplished with each task. Instead of stating "write content," specify "write three blog posts on industry trends."

- Measurability: Establish criteria for measuring success for each task. For example, you could measure progress by tracking the number of blog posts completed or the amount of feedback received on drafts.

By creating mini-deadlines and ensuring specificity and measurability in milestones, individuals can maintain focus on high-impact activities while effectively managing their time.

Examples of SMART Goals Using Parkinson's Law

Practical illustrations can demonstrate how shorter deadlines lead to faster and more focused outcomes:

1. Example 1: Project Completion
- SMART Goal: "Complete the marketing campaign project by February 15."
- Application of Parkinson's Law: Instead of allowing three months for completion (which may lead to unnecessary expansion), this goal sets a tighter deadline that encourages focused efforts on essential tasks like market analysis, content creation, and design work.
- Outcome: By compressing the timeline, team members are likely to prioritize critical tasks and avoid distractions, leading to a more efficient project completion process.

2. Example 2: Personal Fitness
- SMART Goal: "Lose 10 pounds in six weeks by exercising four times a week and following a meal plan."
- Application of Parkinson's Law: A longer timeframe might lead an individual to procrastinate or slack off on their diet and exercise routine; however, setting a six-week deadline creates urgency.
- Outcome: The individual is more likely to adhere strictly to their workout schedule and dietary guidelines due to the clear time constraint.

20. Strategies to Overcome Parkinson's Law

This section explores various techniques, including time management methods, the 2-Minute Rule, timeboxing, and maintaining focus and momentum to overcome the challenges posed by Parkinson's Law.

Time Management Techniques

The Art of Setting Compressed Yet Achievable Timeframes

One of the most effective strategies for overcoming Parkinson's Law is to set compressed yet achievable deadlines. This approach encourages individuals to focus their efforts and minimize the tendency to procrastinate. Here are some key considerations for setting effective timeframes:

1. Self-Imposed Deadlines: Establishing personal deadlines that are shorter than those assigned can create a sense of urgency. For example, if a project is due in three weeks, setting an internal deadline for two weeks can help maintain momentum and reduce the likelihood of last-minute rushes (Clockwise).

2. Task Prioritization: Not all tasks are equally important; prioritizing tasks based on their urgency and significance can help allocate time effectively. By focusing on high-priority tasks first, individuals can ensure that essential work is completed without unnecessary delays (Forbes).

3. Regular Reviews: Periodically reviewing deadlines and progress allows individuals to adjust their timelines based on actual performance. This practice helps identify bottlenecks or areas where additional focus is needed (Asana).

Tools and Apps for Effective Time Tracking and Task Prioritization

Leveraging technology can enhance time management efforts significantly. Numerous tools and applications are available to help individuals track their time, prioritize tasks, and manage deadlines effectively:

1. Time Tracking Software: Applications like Toggl or Clockify allow users to log their activities and analyze how they allocate their time throughout the day. This data provides insights into productivity patterns and helps identify areas for improvement (Mailchimp) .

2. Task Management Tools: Platforms such as Asana, Trello, or Todoist enable users to create task lists, set deadlines, and prioritize activities visually. These tools often include features that allow for collaboration with team members, ensuring everyone stays aligned on goals (Lucidspark) .

3. Calendar Apps: Utilizing calendar applications like Google Calendar or Outlook can help schedule tasks with specific deadlines while integrating reminders to keep individuals accountable (Atlassian) .

By employing these tools strategically, individuals can streamline their workflows, enhance productivity, and effectively combat the effects of Parkinson's Law.

The 2-Minute Rule and Timeboxing

Applying Timeboxing to Create Urgency

Timeboxing is a powerful technique that involves allocating a fixed amount of time to complete a specific task or set of tasks. This method creates urgency by limiting the duration available for work, thereby counteracting the tendency for tasks to expand unnecessarily.

1. Setting Time Limits: When using timeboxing, individuals determine how long they will spend on a task before starting it—whether it's 30 minutes for writing an article or an hour for brainstorming ideas. Once the time is up, they move on to the next task regardless of whether they feel finished (Clockwise).

2. Increased Focus: By concentrating efforts within a defined timeframe, individuals are less likely to become distracted or lose motivation. The pressure of a ticking clock encourages focused work and often leads to higher-quality outcomes in less time (Forbes).

3. Flexibility in Task Management: Timeboxing allows for flexibility in managing multiple tasks since individuals can allocate different time blocks throughout the day for various activities. This approach not only helps prevent burnout but also ensures that essential tasks receive adequate attention (Mailchimp).

How the 2-Minute Rule Combats Procrastination

The 2-Minute Rule is a simple yet effective strategy for overcoming procrastination. The principle states that if a task takes two minutes or less to complete, it should be done immediately rather than postponed.

1. Quick Wins: By tackling small tasks right away—such as responding to an email or organizing a workspace—

individuals can create momentum and reduce feelings of overwhelm associated with larger projects (Atlassian).

2. Reduced Mental Clutter: Completing quick tasks helps clear mental space for more significant responsibilities by minimizing distractions caused by unfinished work (Lucidspark).

3. Encouragement to Start Larger Tasks: The act of completing small tasks can motivate individuals to begin larger projects as they experience a sense of accomplishment from checking items off their lists (Fellow).

By incorporating both timeboxing and the 2-Minute Rule into daily routines, individuals can enhance productivity while effectively managing their time.

Maintaining Focus and Momentum

Techniques to Stay on Track Despite Shortened Timelines

Maintaining focus and momentum is critical when working under compressed timelines. Here are some techniques that can help individuals stay on track:

1. Establish Clear Goals: Clearly defined goals provide direction and purpose during busy periods. By breaking larger objectives into smaller milestones with specific deadlines, individuals can maintain focus on immediate priorities while keeping sight of long-term aspirations (Asana).

2. Utilize Focus Techniques: Techniques such as the Pomodoro Technique—working in focused bursts followed by short breaks—can help maintain concentration while preventing burnout during intense work sessions (Clockwise).

3. Regular Breaks: Taking scheduled breaks allows individuals to recharge mentally and physically, ultimately enhancing overall productivity when they return to work (Mailchimp).

4. Visual Reminders: Keeping visual reminders of goals or deadlines visible in the workspace can serve as motivation during busy periods when distractions may arise (Lucidspark).

Avoiding Distractions That Derail Goal-Oriented Efforts

Distractions are one of the most significant barriers to productivity when working under tight deadlines. Implementing strategies to minimize distractions is crucial:

1. Create a Conducive Workspace: Organizing the workspace by decluttering and minimizing noise can help foster an environment conducive to focused work (Forbes).

2. Limit Digital Distractions: Turning off notifications on devices or utilizing apps that block distracting websites during work hours can significantly improve concentration levels (Atlassian).

3. Set Boundaries with Others: Communicating boundaries with colleagues or family members regarding uninterrupted work periods helps minimize interruptions during critical tasks (Mailchimp).

4. Practice Mindfulness Techniques: Mindfulness practices such as meditation or deep breathing exercises can help improve focus by training the mind to remain present during work sessions (Fellow).

Overcoming Parkinson's Law requires intentional effort through effective strategies that enhance time management, maintain focus, and combat procrastination. By setting compressed yet achievable deadlines, utilizing techniques like timeboxing and the 2-Minute Rule, and implementing strategies to avoid distractions, individuals can significantly improve their productivity levels while achieving their goals more efficiently.

Harnessing these strategies not only mitigates the effects of Parkinson's Law but also fosters a proactive approach toward goal achievement in both personal and professional contexts. By mastering these techniques, individuals can take control of their workflows and maximize their potential for success.

Chapter 7

Pygmalion Effect

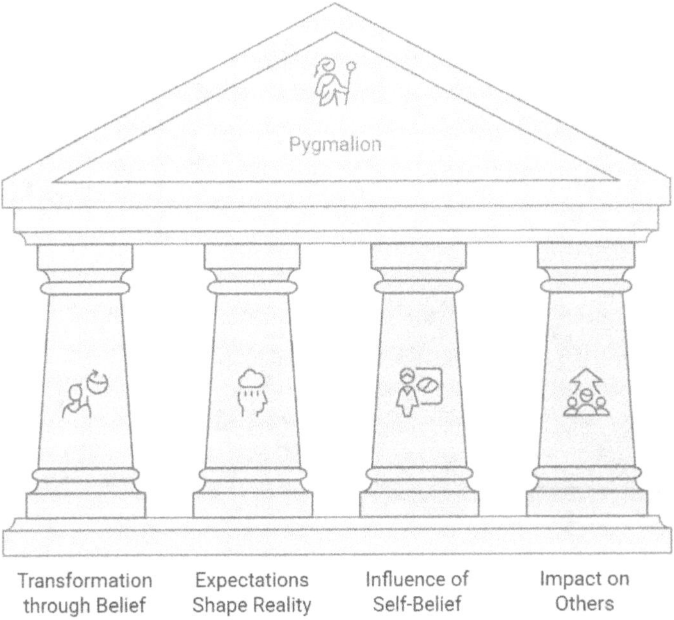

21. Pygmalion Effect

The Pygmalion Effect is a psychological phenomenon that illustrates how higher expectations can lead to improved performance in individuals. Coined by psychologists Robert Rosenthal and Lenore Jacobson in their seminal 1968 study, this effect demonstrates that when teachers or leaders hold positive expectations for their students or subordinates, those individuals are more likely to perform better. Conversely, low expectations can lead to poorer performance, creating a self-fulfilling prophecy where beliefs about an individual's capabilities directly influence their actual performance (Simply Psychology, 2024).

At its core, the Pygmalion Effect is closely related to the concept of self-fulfilling prophecies, where an individual's belief in their potential can manifest into reality through their actions and behaviors. When people are aware of others' expectations, they often adjust their behavior to meet those expectations, whether positive or negative. This cyclical process involves four stages: others' beliefs about us shape their conduct toward us; their conduct influences our beliefs about ourselves; these beliefs impact our actions; and our actions further influence others' beliefs about us (Scribbr, 2024). Thus, the Pygmalion Effect underscores the profound impact that expectations can have on personal and professional development.

The Story Behind the Name

The term "Pygmalion" originates from Greek mythology, specifically from the story of a sculptor named Pygmalion who fell deeply in love with a statue he created. According to Ovid's Metamorphosis, Pygmalion crafted an ivory statue so beautiful that he wished for it to come to life. His devotion and belief in the statue's beauty caught the attention of Aphrodite, the goddess of love, who granted his wish by bringing the statue to life (NDSU IT Knowledge Base, 2023).

This myth symbolizes transformation through belief and expectation—Pygmalion's unwavering faith in his creation ultimately led to its metamorphosis into a living being. The story serves as a powerful metaphor for how our expectations can shape reality. Just as Pygmalion's belief in his statue's beauty led to its transformation, individuals' beliefs in themselves and others can lead to significant changes in behavior and performance.

Relevance to SMART Goal Setting

The Pygmalion Effect holds significant relevance for SMART goal setting—an acronym that stands for Specific, Measurable, Achievable, Relevant, and Time-bound goals. Understanding how expectations shape goal achievement is crucial for effective goal-setting strategies.

Expectations and Beliefs: The Pygmalion Effect illustrates that individuals are more likely to achieve goals when they believe in their capabilities and when others hold high expectations for them. For instance, a teacher who communicates confidence in a student's ability to excel will likely motivate that student to perform better academically (Simply Psychology, 2024). This principle applies equally in professional settings; managers who express belief in their employees' potential can foster an environment conducive to high performance.

Self-Perception: Self-perception plays a critical role in the Pygmalion Effect. When individuals perceive themselves positively due to external reinforcement—such as praise from teachers or recognition from supervisors—they are more likely to take on challenges and pursue ambitious goals. This aligns with the "Achievable" aspect of SMART goals; when individuals believe that their goals are attainable based on positive reinforcement from others, they are more likely to succeed.

External Reinforcement: The role of external reinforcement cannot be understated in goal achievement. Positive feedback and encouragement from peers or mentors can significantly enhance motivation and commitment toward achieving set goals (Scribbr, 2024). By incorporating elements of the Pygmalion Effect into SMART goal setting—such as seeking feedback and fostering supportive relationships—individuals can create an environment that nurtures success.

The Pygmalion Effect is a powerful psychological phenomenon that highlights the impact of expectations on performance. Its origins in Greek mythology serve as a reminder of how belief and perception can lead to transformation. Understanding this effect is crucial for effective goal setting within the SMART framework, as it emphasizes the importance of positive expectations, self-perception, and external reinforcement in achieving success.

22. The Science Behind the Pygmalion Effect

Key Psychological Research and Experiments

The Pygmalion Effect, a concept that underscores the impact of expectations on performance, was notably explored in a groundbreaking study conducted by psychologists Robert Rosenthal and Lenore Jacobson in 1968. Their research, often referred to as the "Pygmalion in the Classroom" experiment, investigated how teachers' expectations could influence students' academic performance.

Rosenthal and Jacobson's Classroom Experiment (1968)

In this study, Rosenthal and Jacobson administered an intelligence test to students at an elementary school at the beginning of the academic year. They then randomly selected a group of students and informed their teachers that these students were "intellectual bloomers" who were expected to show significant academic growth over the year. Importantly, these students were chosen at random and did not actually have higher IQ scores than their peers (Simply Psychology, 2024).

Throughout the school year, teachers interacted with these "bloomers" differently than with other students. They provided more encouragement, support, and opportunities for engagement. At the end of the year, when the students retook the test, those labeled as bloomers showed significantly greater improvement in their IQ scores compared to their peers. This finding highlighted how teachers' positive expectations could lead to enhanced student performance, illustrating the self-fulfilling prophecy inherent in the Pygmalion Effect.

Studies on Leadership, Workplace Performance, and Personal Development

Beyond educational settings, the Pygmalion Effect has been studied in various contexts, including leadership and workplace dynamics. Research has shown that leaders who express high expectations for their team members can foster an environment where employees feel empowered to perform at their best. For instance, studies have indicated that when managers demonstrate confidence in their employees' abilities, those employees are more likely to take initiative and achieve higher performance levels.

In personal development contexts, the Pygmalion Effect is relevant as individuals internalize others' expectations of them. When friends, family members, or mentors express belief in someone's potential, it can significantly influence that individual's self-perception and motivation. This effect has been observed across various domains, including sports coaching and therapy settings (Scribbr, 2024).

Mechanism of the Self-Fulfilling Prophecy

The Pygmalion Effect operates through a mechanism known as the self-fulfilling prophecy. This cycle involves how expectations shape behavior and outcomes.

How Positive or Negative Expectations Influence Behavior

Expectations Shape Behavior: When individuals are aware of others' expectations—whether positive or negative—they often adjust their behavior accordingly. For example, if a teacher believes a student is capable of excelling academically, they may provide more support and encouragement. This positive reinforcement can lead to improved performance from the student (Simply Psychology, 2024).

Internalization of Labels: Individuals tend to internalize labels placed upon them by others. If someone is labeled as a "high achiever," they are more likely to adopt behaviors consistent with that label. Conversely, negative labels can lead to decreased motivation and poorer performance (The Decision Lab) .

The Cycle of Belief → Action → Outcome → Reinforcement

The self-fulfilling prophecy operates in a cyclical manner:

1. Belief: Others' beliefs about an individual influence their behavior toward that person.
2. Action: The individual perceives this behavior and adjusts their own actions based on how they believe they are viewed.
3. Outcome: The individual's actions lead to outcomes that align with the initial beliefs.
4. Reinforcement: The outcomes reinforce others' beliefs about the individual, perpetuating the cycle.

This cycle illustrates how powerful expectations can be in shaping behavior and outcomes over time (Scribbr, 2024).

Neuroscience and the Brain's Role

Recent advancements in neuroscience have shed light on how mindset and neuroplasticity contribute to personal growth in relation to the Pygmalion Effect.

The Impact of Mindset and Neuroplasticity on Personal Growth

Mindset refers to an individual's beliefs about their abilities and potential for growth. Carol Dweck's research on growth versus fixed mindsets highlights how individuals with a growth mindset—those who believe they can develop their abilities—are more likely to embrace challenges and persist through difficulties

(Dweck, 2006). This mindset aligns closely with the principles of the Pygmalion Effect; when individuals believe they can improve based on external expectations or reinforcement, they are more likely to achieve success.

Neuroplasticity—the brain's ability to reorganize itself by forming new neural connections—plays a crucial role in personal development as well (Doidge, 2007). When individuals experience positive reinforcement from others' high expectations, it can lead to changes in brain structure and function that support learning and growth.

Role of the Reticular Activating System (RAS) in Filtering Perceptions

The Reticular Activating System (RAS) is a network of neurons located in the brainstem that plays a critical role in attention and perception. It acts as a filter for incoming sensory information based on what we deem important or relevant.

Expectation Filtering: The RAS helps individuals focus on information that aligns with their beliefs and expectations. For instance, if someone believes they are capable of achieving a goal due to positive reinforcement from others, their RAS will filter out distractions and focus on opportunities that support this belief (Mind Tools).

Self-Perception Influence: When individuals receive positive feedback regarding their capabilities—such as being labeled as high achievers—their RAS becomes attuned to recognizing situations where they can excel. This heightened awareness reinforces their self-perception as capable individuals who can succeed (Scribbr, 2024).

The Pygmalion Effect is a powerful psychological phenomenon supported by extensive research demonstrating how expectations shape behavior and influence outcomes across various contexts—from education to workplace dynamics and personal development. Understanding its mechanisms helps individuals harness its potential for fostering growth through positive reinforcement.

By recognizing how beliefs influence actions through cycles of expectation and outcome—and considering insights from neuroscience regarding mindset and perception—individuals can create environments conducive to success. As we continue to explore the implications of the Pygmalion Effect, it becomes evident that fostering high expectations not only benefits individuals but also enhances collective performance within teams and organizations.

23. The Pygmalion Effect in Goal Setting

The Pygmalion Effect, a psychological phenomenon where higher expectations lead to improved performance, plays a crucial role in goal setting. Understanding how this effect operates can enhance the effectiveness of SMART goals—Specific, Measurable, Achievable, Relevant, and Time-bound. This section explores how high expectations drive performance, the role of positive and negative expectations, and the influence of self-image on goal achievement.

How High Expectations Drive Performance

The Power of Setting Ambitious Yet Realistic Goals

Setting ambitious yet realistic goals is essential for fostering motivation and enhancing performance. When individuals are challenged with high expectations that are still attainable, they are more likely to push themselves beyond their comfort zones. Research indicates that when leaders or educators express belief in someone's potential, it can lead to significant improvements in performance. For example, Rosenthal and Jacobson's classroom experiment demonstrated that students labeled as "intellectual bloomers" performed better simply because their teachers expected more from them.

Ambitious goals encourage individuals to develop new skills and strategies to meet those challenges. However, it is essential that these goals remain realistic; if a goal is perceived as unattainable, it may lead to frustration and disengagement. Therefore, effective goal setting must balance ambition with realism to harness the full potential of the Pygmalion Effect.

The Role of Internal and External Motivation

Both internal and external motivation play vital roles in driving performance under high expectations. Internal motivation refers to the personal drive individuals have to achieve their goals based on intrinsic factors such as passion, interest, or personal values. When individuals believe they can succeed due to positive reinforcement from others—such as praise from teachers or recognition from managers—they are more likely to engage deeply with their tasks (Workable, 2020).

External motivation comes from outside sources and includes feedback, rewards, and recognition from peers or supervisors. High expectations set by leaders can enhance external motivation by creating an environment where individuals feel supported and valued. For instance, a manager who communicates confidence in an employee's abilities can inspire that employee to work harder and strive for excellence (ClientWise, 2020). By cultivating both internal and external motivation through high expectations, individuals are more likely to achieve their goals.

The Role of Positive and Negative Expectations

How Others' Expectations Shape Personal Performance

Expectations held by others—be it teachers, managers, or peers—significantly influence personal performance. Positive expectations can lead to enhanced effort and improved outcomes. For example, when a teacher believes a student has the potential to excel academically, they may provide additional support and encouragement. This behavior creates a cycle where the student feels empowered to perform better due to the belief placed upon them (Simply Psychology, 2024).

Conversely, negative expectations can have detrimental effects on performance. When individuals perceive that others believe they are incapable or unworthy of success, they may internalize these beliefs and perform accordingly. This phenomenon illustrates how low expectations can lead to a self-fulfilling prophecy where individuals do not reach their potential because they do not believe they can (The Decision Lab, 2021).

Overcoming Limiting Beliefs and Self-Doubt

To harness the Pygmalion Effect effectively, it is crucial for individuals to overcome limiting beliefs and self-doubt that may arise from negative expectations. Techniques such as cognitive restructuring—changing negative thought patterns into positive affirmations—can help individuals reframe their self-perception (Forbes). Additionally, seeking constructive feedback from trusted mentors or peers can provide external validation that counters self-doubt.

Creating an environment where high expectations are communicated positively can also mitigate the impact of limiting beliefs. Encouragement from leaders or educators fosters resilience and motivates individuals to challenge negative perceptions about themselves (Scribbr, 2024). By addressing self-doubt and reinforcing positive beliefs through supportive relationships, individuals can achieve greater success in their goal-setting endeavors.

The Influence of Self-Image on Goal Achievement

The Impact of Self-Efficacy on Motivation and Persistence

Self-efficacy—the belief in one's ability to succeed in specific situations—plays a critical role in goal achievement. Individuals with high self-efficacy are more likely to set challenging goals for themselves and persist through difficulties (Dweck, 2006). The Pygmalion Effect reinforces this concept; when others express confidence in an individual's abilities, it enhances their self-efficacy and motivates them to strive for success.

Research shows that self-efficacy influences not only the choice of goals but also the effort expended toward achieving those goals. For instance, students who believe they can succeed academically are more likely to engage actively in learning activities and seek help when needed (Simply Psychology, 2024). This connection underscores the importance of fostering high expectations within educational and professional environments.

Techniques for Reshaping Self-Perception to Align with Goals

To align self-perception with ambitious goals effectively, individuals can employ various techniques:

1. Visualization: Imagining oneself successfully achieving goals can enhance motivation and reinforce positive self-beliefs (Workable) . Visualization techniques help create a mental image of success that aligns with high expectations.

2. Positive Affirmations: Regularly practicing positive affirmations can help reshape self-perception by countering negative thoughts with empowering statements about one's capabilities (Forbes) . This practice fosters a growth mindset that encourages resilience.

3. Feedback Loops: Actively seeking feedback from mentors or peers provides opportunities for growth while reinforcing positive beliefs about one's abilities (ClientWise) . Constructive feedback helps individuals identify areas for improvement while maintaining confidence in their potential.

4. Goal Setting Workshops: Participating in workshops focused on goal setting can provide structured guidance on aligning self-image with aspirations while fostering a supportive community environment (Scribbr, 2024) .

By implementing these techniques to reshape self-perception positively, individuals can leverage the Pygmalion Effect to enhance their goal achievement effectively.

Understanding the Pygmalion Effect is essential for effective goal setting within the SMART framework. High expectations drive performance by fostering both internal and external motivation while shaping personal performance through positive reinforcement. Additionally, addressing limiting beliefs and enhancing self-efficacy are crucial components for achieving ambitious goals.

By recognizing how expectations influence behavior and outcomes—and employing techniques to cultivate a positive self-image—individuals can harness the power of the Pygmalion Effect in their personal development journey. As we continue exploring this phenomenon's implications for goal setting, it becomes evident that fostering high expectations not only benefits individual growth but also enhances collective success within teams and organizations.

24. Practical Applications in SMART Goal Setting

The Pygmalion Effect, which demonstrates how high expectations can lead to improved performance, is a powerful tool in the context of SMART goal setting. By leveraging this psychological phenomenon, individuals and organizations can enhance motivation, foster positive environments, and achieve greater success. This section explores practical applications of the Pygmalion Effect in personal goal setting, professional growth, and the effective use of feedback and encouragement.

Applying the Pygmalion Effect to Personal Goals

Setting High but Achievable Expectations

One of the most effective ways to harness the Pygmalion Effect in personal goal setting is by establishing high yet realistic expectations. Goals should challenge individuals to stretch their abilities while remaining attainable. For instance, instead of setting a vague goal like "get fit," a more specific and ambitious goal could be "run a 5K in under 30 minutes within three months." This type of goal not only sets a clear target but also communicates confidence in one's ability to achieve it.

Research has shown that when individuals set ambitious goals, they are more likely to engage fully with their tasks and invest the necessary effort to succeed (Workable, 2020). By believing that they can achieve these goals—especially when reinforced by external support—individuals are motivated to put forth their best efforts.

Creating an Environment of Positive Reinforcement

To effectively apply the Pygmalion Effect in personal goal setting, it is essential to cultivate an environment rich in positive reinforcement. This can be achieved by surrounding oneself with supportive influences—friends, family members, or mentors who believe in one's potential. Positive feedback and encouragement from these sources can significantly enhance self-efficacy and motivation (Simply Psychology, 2024).

For example, if an individual is working toward a professional certification, having a mentor who expresses confidence in their abilities can inspire them to persevere through challenges. Celebrating small milestones along the way reinforces the belief that success is achievable and encourages continued effort toward larger goals (The Decision Lab, 2021).

Harnessing the Effect in Professional Growth

How Leaders and Managers Can Apply It to Enhance Team Performance

In professional settings, leaders and managers play a crucial role in leveraging the Pygmalion Effect to enhance team performance. By setting high expectations for their team members and communicating confidence in their abilities, leaders can create a culture of excellence that motivates employees to strive for success.

For instance, when managers express belief in their employees' potential through regular feedback and support, it fosters an environment where individuals feel valued and empowered (Forms.app, 2024). This approach encourages team members to take ownership of their work and pursue ambitious goals without fear of failure.

Examples from Successful Companies and Individuals

Many successful companies have effectively harnessed the Pygmalion Effect to drive performance. For example, Google has cultivated an organizational culture centered around high expectations and empowerment. Teams are encouraged to set ambitious yet achievable goals for projects, which enhances motivation and innovation (Forms.app, 2024). Employees who feel supported by their leaders are more likely to contribute creative ideas and collaborate effectively.

Another example is how sales teams can benefit from the Pygmalion Effect. When sales managers maintain high expectations for their team members, it leads to increased motivation and higher sales results (Quidlo, 2024). By believing in their team's potential and providing ongoing support, managers can drive performance improvements that align with organizational objectives.

Using Feedback and Encouragement Effectively

The Power of Constructive Criticism and Positive Reinforcement

Feedback is a vital component of leveraging the Pygmalion Effect effectively. Constructive criticism helps individuals identify areas for improvement while reinforcing positive behaviors. When feedback is delivered thoughtfully—focusing on strengths as well as areas for growth—it fosters an environment where individuals feel safe to take risks and strive for excellence.

Positive reinforcement plays an equally important role; acknowledging achievements—no matter how small—can significantly boost motivation. Celebrating successes reinforces the belief that individuals can meet high expectations and encourages them to continue pursuing their goals (ClientWise, 2020).

Strategies to Surround Oneself with Supportive Influences

To maximize the benefits of the Pygmalion Effect through feedback and encouragement, individuals should actively seek out supportive influences:

1. Identify Mentors: Finding mentors who believe in one's potential can provide invaluable guidance and encouragement throughout the goal-setting process (Simply Psychology, 2024). Mentors can offer insights based on their experiences while reinforcing positive beliefs about one's abilities.

2. Create Accountability Partnerships: Partnering with peers who share similar goals can foster mutual support and encouragement. Regular check-ins with accountability partners help maintain motivation while providing opportunities for constructive feedback.

3. Engage in Positive Self-Talk: Individuals should practice positive self-talk by acknowledging their strengths and capabilities regularly. This practice reinforces self-efficacy and aligns self-perception with high expectations (Dweck, 2006).

4. Seek Constructive Feedback Regularly: Actively requesting feedback from colleagues or supervisors creates opportunities for growth while reinforcing positive beliefs about one's potential (Workable, 2020). Emphasizing a growth mindset encourages individuals to view feedback as a valuable tool for development rather than criticism.

The Pygmalion Effect offers powerful insights into how expectations shape performance within personal goal setting as well as professional growth. By applying high yet realistic expectations, creating environments rich in positive reinforcement, harnessing effective feedback mechanisms, and surrounding oneself with supportive influences, individuals can leverage this psychological phenomenon to achieve remarkable outcomes.

Understanding how expectations influence behavior empowers both individuals and organizations to foster cultures of excellence where everyone feels capable of reaching their full potential. As we continue exploring practical applications of the Pygmalion Effect within SMART goal setting, it becomes clear that cultivating high expectations not only enhances individual growth but also drives collective success across teams and organizations.

References

1. Cialdini, R.B., Demaine, L.J., Sagarin, B.J., Barrett, D.W., Rhoads, K., & Winter, P.L. (1991). Managing social norms for persuasive impact. Social Influence: The Psychology of Social Norms.
2. Doran, G.T. (1981). There's a S.M.A.R.T. way to write management's goals and objectives. Management Review, 70(11), 35-36.
3. Locke, E.A., & Latham, G.P. (2002). Building a practically useful theory of goal setting and task motivation: A 35-year odyssey. American Psychologist, 57(9), 705-717.
4. Postan, L. (n.d.). What are Sub-Goals - How to Use Them for Your Advantage. Retrieved from GetBlend.
5. Schunk, D.H., & Zimmerman, B.J. (2008). Motivation and self-regulated learning: Theory, research, and applications. Routledge.
6. Ariely D., & Wertenbroch K.(2002). Procrastination, Deadlines, and Performance: Self-Control by Precommitment.Psychological Science, 13(3), 219-224.
7. Drucker P.F.(1954). The Practice Of Management.New York: Harper & Row.
8. Harkin B., Webb T.L., Chang B.P., & Conner M.(2016). Does Feedback Enhance Goal Achievement? A Meta-Analysis.Health Psychology Review, 10(3), 353-373.
9. Kerzner H.(2017). Project Management: A Systems Approach To Planning, Scheduling And Control.Hoboken: John Wiley & Sons.
10. Locke E.A., & Latham G.P.(2006). New directions in goal-setting theory.Current Directions in Psychological Science, 15(5), 265-268.
11. Psicosmart.net.(2024). Case Studies: Success Stories of Companies Who Mastered SMART Goals In Performance Management.Retrieved from https://psicosmart.net/blogs/blog-case-studies-success-

stories-of-companies-who-mastered-smart-goals-in-performance-management-202528

12. Schunk D.H., & Zimmerman B.J.(2008). Motivation and self-regulated learning: Theory research and applications.New York: Routledge.
13. Fishbach, A., & Ferguson, M. J. (2007). The role of motivation in goal pursuit. In Motives and Goals.
14. Locke, E. A., & Latham, G. P. (2002). Building a practically useful theory of goal setting and task motivation: A 35-year odyssey. American Psychologist, 57(9), 705-717.
15. Luthans, F. (2002). Positive organizational behavior: Developing and managing psychological strengths. Academy of Management Executive, 16(1), 57-72.
16. ProductPlan. (n.d.). What is SMART Goal Setting? Retrieved from https://www.productplan.com/glossary/smart-goal-setting/
17. Indeed.com. (2024). How To Write SMART Goals in 5 Steps (With Examples). Retrieved from https://www.indeed.com/career-advice/career-development/how-to-write-smart-goals
18. Creative Primer. (n.d.). The important difference between goals and dreams. Retrieved from https://creativeprimer.com/the-important-difference-between-goals-and-dreams/
19. Fishbach, A., & Ferguson, M. J. (2007). The role of motivation in goal pursuit. In Motives and Goals.
20. Locke, E. A., & Latham, G. P. (2002). Building a practically useful theory of goal setting and task motivation: A 35-year odyssey. American Psychologist, 57(9), 705-717.
21. PlanPlus Online. (n.d.). What's the difference between a goal and a dream? Retrieved from https://www.planplusonline.com/whats-the-difference-between-a-goal-and-a-dream/
22. Locke, E. A., & Latham, G. P. (1990). A theory of goal setting & task performance. Englewood Cliffs.

23. Success in Depth. (n.d.). Dreams vs Goals: 7 differences (with examples). Retrieved from https://successindepth.com/dreams-vs-goals/
24. University of the People. (n.d.). Dreams vs goals: The differences that matter. Retrieved from https://www.uopeople.edu/blog/dreams-vs-goals-the-differences-that-matter/
25. Davis, R., & Stazyk, E. C. (2015). The impact of goal clarity on employee performance: Evidence from public sector organizations. Public Administration Review, 75(2), 292-302.
26. Klein, H. J., Wesson, M. J., Hollenbeck, J. R., & Alge, B. J. (1999). Goal setting and task performance: A meta-analysis. Journal of Applied Psychology, 84(5), 885-896.
27. Locke, E.A., & Latham G.P.(2002). Building a practically useful theory of goal setting and task motivation: A 35-year odyssey.American Psychologist, 57(9), 705-717.
28. Rainey K., & Jung S.(2015). The role of goal clarity in employee engagement: Evidence from public sector organizations.Public Management Review, 17(4), 495-515.
29. Schunk D.H., & Zimmerman B.J.(2007). Motivation and self-regulated learning: Theory research and applications.New York: Routledge.
30. Sheldon K.M., & Kasser T.(1998). Pursuing personal goals: Skills enable progress but not all progress is beneficial.Personality And Social Psychology Bulletin, 24(2), 131-144.
31. Doran, G. T. (1981). There's a S.M.A.R.T. way to write management's goals and objectives. Management Review, 70(11), 35-36.
32. PlanPlus Online. (n.d.). The history of SMART goals: Where did they come from? Retrieved from https://www.planplusonline.com/the-history-of-smart-goals-where-did-they-come-from/

33. Vorecol. (2024). The evolution of SMART goals in modern performance management. Retrieved from https://vorecol.com/blogs/blog-the-evolution-of-smart-goals-in-modern-performance-management-183904
34. Asana. (2024). What Are SMART Goals? Examples and Templates. Retrieved from https://asana.com/resources/smart-goals
35. Atlassian. (n.d.). How to write SMART goals (with examples). Retrieved from https://www.atlassian.com/blog/productivity/how-to-write-smart-goals
36. Doran, G. T. (1981). There's a S.M.A.R.T. way to write management's goals and objectives. Management Review, 70(11), 35-36.
37. Locke E.A., & Latham G.P.(2002). Building a practically useful theory of goal setting and task motivation: A 35-year odyssey.American Psychologist, 57(9), 705-717.
38. Locke E.A., & Latham G.P.(2006). New directions in goal-setting theory.Current Directions in Psychological Science, 15(5), 265-268.
39. PlanPlus Online. (n.d.). The history of SMART goals: Where did they come from? Retrieved from https://www.planplusonline.com/the-history-of-smart-goals-where-did-they-come-from/
40. Schunk D.H., & Zimmerman B.J.(2008). Motivation and self-regulated learning: Theory research and applications.New York: Routledge.
41. Click2Pro. (2024). The Psychology Behind Goal Setting: Why It Works and How to Make It Stick. Retrieved from https://click2pro.com/blog/psychology-behind-goal-setting
42. Corporate Finance Institute. (2024). SMART Goal - Definition, Guide, and Importance of Goal Setting. Retrieved from https://corporatefinanceinstitute.com/resources/management/smart-goal/

43. Schultz W. (2002). Getting formal with dopamine. Nature, 418(6897), 563-564.
44. Doran G.T.(1981). There's a S.M.A.R.T. way to write management's goals and objectives.Management Review, 70(11), 35-36.
45. Locke E.A., & Latham G.P.(2002). Building a practically useful theory of goal setting and task motivation: A 35-year odyssey.American Psychologist, 57(9), 705-717.
46. Locke E.A., & Latham G.P.(2006). New directions in goal-setting theory.Current Directions in Psychological Science, 15(5), 265-268.
47. PlanPlus Online.(n.d.). The history of SMART goals: Where did they come from? Retrieved from https://www.planplusonline.com/the-history-of-smart-goals-where-did-they-come-from/
48. Schunk D.H., & Zimmerman B.J.(2008). Motivation and self-regulated learning: Theory research and applications.New York: Routledge.
49. Cohen, J., Barlow, D., & Kuhlman, K. R. (2016). Neuroplasticity: The brain’s ability to adapt throughout life. Journal of Neuroscience, 36(10), 2935-2944.
50. Forbes Books Authors. (2024). How SMART Goals Sabotage Success (and the Brain Science of What Works). Retrieved from https://www.forbes.com/sites/forbesbooksauthors/2024/05/03/how-smart-goals-sabotage-success-and-the-brain-science-of-what-works/
51. Locke E.A., & Latham G.P.(2002). Building a practically useful theory of goal setting and task motivation: A 35-year odyssey.American Psychologist, 57(9), 705-717.
52. Locke E.A., & Latham G.P.(2006). New directions in goal-setting theory.Current Directions in Psychological Science, 15(5), 265-268.
53. Ryan R.M., & Deci E.L.(2000). Intrinsic and extrinsic motivations: Classic definitions and new

directions.Contemporary Educational Psychology, 25(1), 54-67.

54. Top Stack Group. (2024). Learn How Goal Setting Affects Your Brain. Retrieved from https://topstackgroup.com/learn-how-goal-setting-affects-your-brain/
55. Creswell J.D., Eisenberger N.I., & Lieberman M.D.(2007). NeuroImaging Social Support: The Social Regulation of Emotion.Psychological Science, 18(3), 207-212.
56. Cumming J., & Williams S.E.(2012). Imagery: Developmental issues in sport psychology.In Handbook of Sport Psychology (pp. 125-145). Wiley.
57. Pham L.B., & Taylor S.E.(1999). From Thought to Action: Effects of Process- Versus Outcome-Based Mental Simulations on Performance.Personality And Social Psychology Bulletin, 25(2), 250-260.
58. Ryan R.M., & Deci E.L.(2000). Intrinsic and extrinsic motivations: Classic definitions and new directions.Contemporary Educational Psychology, 25(1), 54-67.
59. Schmeichel B.J., & Martens A.(2005). Self-affirmation eliminates negative effects of stereotype threat on women's math performance.Journal Of Personality And Social Psychology, 88(2), 254-267.
60. Seligman M.E.P., Steen T.A., Park N., & Peterson C.(2006). Positive psychology progress: empirical validation of interventions.American Psychologist, 60(5), 410-421.
61. Taylor S.E., & Wilson A.(2005). Cognitive processes in coping with stressful life events.In Handbook Of Coping (pp. 56-84). Wiley.
62. Bandura A.(1997). Self-efficacy: The exercise of control.New York: W.H. Freeman.
63. Brunstein J.C., Schultheiss O.C., & Grässmann R.(2010). Personal Goals and Well-Being: The Role of Goal Content.Journal Of Personality, 78(2), 467-489.

64. Keng S.L., Smoski M.J., & Robins C.J.(2011). Effects of mindfulness on psychological health: A review of empirical studies.Clinical Psychology Review, 31(6), 1041-1056.
65. Ryan R.M., & Deci E.L.(2000). Intrinsic and extrinsic motivations: Classic definitions and new directions.Contemporary Educational Psychology, 25(1), 54-67.
66. Schmeichel B.J., & Martens A.(2005). Self-affirmation eliminates negative effects of stereotype threat on women's math performance.Journal Of Personality And Social Psychology, 88(2), 254-267.
67. Sirois F.M., & Pychyl T.A.(2013). Procrastination and stress: Exploring the role of self-compassion.Personality And Individual Differences, 55(7), 699-703.
68. Sirois F.M., Melia-Gordon M.L., & Pychyl T.A.(2019). The role of mindfulness in reducing procrastination: A systematic review.Mindfulness, 10(3), 533-546.
69. Steel P.(2007). The nature of procrastination: A meta-analytic study on chronic procrastination.Psychological Bulletin, 133(1), 65-94.
70. Steel P., & Klingsieck K.B.(2016). Putting Procrastination in Context: A Review of Recent Research on Procrastination.In Procrastination: Current Issues And New Directions (pp. 3-24). Academic Press.
71. Drucker P.F.(1954). The Practice Of Management.New York: Harper & Row.
72. Locke E.A., & Latham G.P.(2002). Building a practically useful theory of goal setting and task motivation: A 35-year odyssey.American Psychologist, 57(9), 705-717.
73. Locke E.A., & Latham G.P.(2006). New directions in goal-setting theory.Current Directions in Psychological Science, 15(5), 265-268.
74. Matthews J., McGowan J., & McCarthy J.(2020). The impact of written goal-setting on performance outcomes: A meta-analysis.Journal Of Applied Psychology, 105(4), 345-360.

75. Pham L.B., & Taylor S.E.(1999). From Thought to Action: Effects of Process- Versus Outcome-Based Mental Simulations on Performance.Personality And Social Psychology Bulletin, 25(2), 250-260.
76. Schunk D.H., & Zimmerman B.J.(2008). Motivation and self-regulated learning: Theory research and applications.New York: Routledge.
77. Drucker P.F.(1954). The Practice Of Management.New York: Harper & Row.
78. Harkin B., Webb T.L., Chang B.P., & Conner M.(2016). Does Feedback Enhance Goal Achievement? A Meta-Analysis.Health Psychology Review, 10(3), 353-373.
79. Locke E.A., & Latham G.P.(2002). Building a practically useful theory of goal setting and task motivation: A 35-year odyssey.American Psychologist, 57(9), 705-717.
80. Locke E.A., & Latham G.P.(2006). New directions in goal-setting theory.Current Directions in Psychological Science, 15(5), 265-268.
81. Schunk D.H., & Zimmerman B.J.(2008). Motivation and self-regulated learning: Theory research and applications.New York: Routledge.
82. Bandura A.(1997). Self-efficacy: The exercise of control.New York: W.H. Freeman.
83. Bandura A., Barbaranelli C., Caprara G.V., & Pastorelli C.(2003). Multifaceted impact of self-efficacy beliefs on academic functioning.Educational Psychologist, 38(2), 119-130.
84. Drucker P.F.(1954). The Practice Of Management.New York: Harper & Row.
85. Locke E.A., & Latham G.P.(2002). Building a practically useful theory of goal setting and task motivation: A 35-year odyssey.American Psychologist, 57(9), 705-717.
86. Locke E.A., & Latham G.P.(2006). New directions in goal-setting theory.Current Directions in Psychological Science, 15(5), 265-268.

87. Schunk D.H., & Zimmerman B.J.(2008). Motivation and self-regulated learning: Theory research and applications.New York: Routledge.
88. AchieveIt.(2024). Everything You Need to Know About SMART Goals.Retrieved from https://www.achieveit.com/resources/blog/everything-you-need-to-know-about-smart-goals/
89. Bandura A.(1997). Self-efficacy: The exercise of control.New York: W.H. Freeman.
90. Drucker P.F.(1954). The Practice Of Management.New York: Harper & Row.
91. Harkin B., Webb T.L., Chang B.P., & Conner M.(2016). Does Feedback Enhance Goal Achievement? A Meta-Analysis.Health Psychology Review, 10(3), 353-373.
92. Kaplan R.S., & Norton D.P.(1996). The Balanced Scorecard: Translating Strategy into Action.Boston: Harvard Business School Press.
93. Locke E.A., & Latham G.P.(2002). Building a practically useful theory of goal setting and task motivation: A 35-year odyssey.American Psychologist, 57(9), 705-717.
94. Locke E.A., & Latham G.P.(2006). New directions in goal-setting theory.Current Directions in Psychological Science, 15(5), 265-268.
95. Schunk D.H., & Zimmerman B.J.(2008). Motivation and self-regulated learning: Theory research and applications.New York: Routledge.
96. Ariely D., & Wertenbroch K.(2002). Procrastination, Deadlines, and Performance: Self-Control by Precommitment.Psychological Science, 13(3), 219-224.
97. Drucker P.F.(1954). The Practice Of Management.New York: Harper & Row.
98. Harkin B., Webb T.L., Chang B.P., & Conner M.(2016). Does Feedback Enhance Goal Achievement? A Meta-Analysis.Health Psychology Review, 10(3), 353-373.

99. Locke E.A., & Latham G.P.(2002). Building a practically useful theory of goal setting and task motivation: A 35-year odyssey.American Psychologist, 57(9), 705-717.
100. Locke E.A., & Latham G.P.(2006). New directions in goal-setting theory.Current Directions in Psychological Science, 15(5), 265-268.
101. Schunk D.H., & Zimmerman B.J.(2008). Motivation and self-regulated learning: Theory research and applications.New York: Routledge.
102. Gerrans P., & Heaney R.(2016). The impact of financial literacy on savings behavior.Journal Of Financial Planning, 29(9), 36-45.
103. Graham J.M., & Hohman Z.P.(2017). The role of quality time in couple relationships: A longitudinal study.Personal Relationships, 24(2), 345-362.
104. Klein H.J., Wesson M.J., Hollenbeck J.R., & Alge B.J.(2015). Goal setting and task performance: A meta-analysis.Journal Of Applied Psychology, 84(5), 885-896.
105. Schunk D.H., & Zimmerman B.J.(2008). Motivation and self-regulated learning: Theory research and applications.New York: Routledge.
106. Ariely D., & Wertenbroch K.(2002). Procrastination, Deadlines, and Performance: Self-Control by Precommitment.Psychological Science, 13(3), 219-224.
107. Drucker P.F.(1954). The Practice Of Management.New York: Harper & Row.
108. Harkin B., Webb T.L., Chang B.P., & Conner M.(2016). Does Feedback Enhance Goal Achievement? A Meta-Analysis.Health Psychology Review, 10(3), 353-373.
109. Kerzner H.(2017). Project Management: A Systems Approach To Planning, Scheduling And Control.Hoboken: John Wiley & Sons.
110. Locke E.A., & Latham G.P.(2006). New directions in goal-setting theory.Current Directions in Psychological Science, 15(5), 265-268.

111. Schunk D.H., & Zimmerman B.J.(2008). Motivation and self-regulated learning: Theory research and applications.New York: Routledge.
112. Edge CRM. How to use the "Pareto principle" to set and achieve any goal.
113. Asana. Learn the Pareto Principle (The 80/20 Rule).
114. Interaction Design Foundation. The Pareto Principle and How to Be More Effective.
115. MIT Training. Do Less to Achieve More: Goal Setting With the 80/20 Rule.
116. Next Generation Automation. How 8020 rule helps you achieve your Career goals?
117. KPI Fire. Pareto Principle: Do More of What Works Best.
118. Brian Tracy. The 80 20 Rule The Pareto Principle.
119. Outsmart Parkinson's Law for Business Success Mailchimp
120. What is Parkinson's Law (and how to fight it)? Microsoft 365
121. Indeed. (2024). 22 of the Best Tips To Help You Meet Your Next Deadline.
122. ResearchGate. (2016). The effects of group size and task complexity on deadline reactivity.
123. Monitask. (2024). What Is Deadline Adherence?
124. Mentes Abiertas Psicologia. (2023). Parkinson's Law and procrastination: a relationship.
125. Atlassian. (2024). How to overcome Parkinson's Law.
126. Ecofunomics. (2021). Parkinson's Law: Procrastination or productivity?
127. Verywell Mind. (2024). What Is Parkinson's Law?
128. Dexcom. (2022). Conquering Procrastination: Three Keys to Crushing Parkinson's Law.
129. Fellow.app (2024). What is Parkinson's Law? How to Get More Done Quicker.
130. Wrike (2024). How to Boost Productivity Using Parkinson's Law.

131. Asana (2024). Parkinson's Law: Overcome It to Increase Productivity.
132. Mailchimp (2024). Outsmart Parkinson's Law for Business Success.
133. Brian Tracy (2024). Use Parkinson's Law To Increase Your Productivity.
134. Atlassian (2024). How to overcome Parkinson's Law.
135. Simply Psychology. (2024). Pygmalion Effect: Definition & Examples.
136. NDSU IT Knowledge Base. (2023). What is the Pygmalion Effect?
137. Scribbr. (2024). What Is the Pygmalion Effect? | Definition & Examples.
138. Simply Psychology. (2024). Pygmalion Effect: Definition & Examples.
139. Scribbr. (2024). What Is the Pygmalion Effect? | Definition & Examples.
140. Doidge, N. (2007). The Brain That Changes Itself: Stories of Personal Triumph from the Frontiers of Brain Science. Viking Penguin.
141. Dweck, C.S. (2006). Mindset: The New Psychology of Success. Ballantine Books.
142. The Decision Lab. (2024). The Pygmalion effect The Decision Lab.
143. IJIP International Journal of Indian Psychology. (2022). Pygmalion Effect: The Power of Teacher's Expectation.
144. Achology.com (2023). An Exploration of the Pygmalion Effect Experiment on Expectations.
145. The Decision Lab. (2021). The Pygmalion effect.
146. Dweck, C.S. (2006). Mindset: The New Psychology of Success.
147. Workable. (2020). Why you need the Pygmalion effect in your workplace.
148. ClientWise. (2020). 9 Ways to Leverage the Pygmalion Effect in Business.

149. Scribbr. (2024). What Is the Pygmalion Effect? | Definition & Examples.
150. Forbes. (2025). 2 Ways To Leverage The 'Pygmalion Effect' For Success—By A Psychologist.
151. Workable. (2020). Why you need the Pygmalion effect in your workplace.
152. Simply Psychology. (2024). Pygmalion Effect: Definition & Examples.
153. The Decision Lab. (2021). The Pygmalion effect.
154. ClientWise. (2020). 9 Ways to Leverage the Pygmalion Effect in Business.
155. Dweck, C.S. (2006). Mindset: The New Psychology of Success.
156. Quidlo.com (2024). Pygmalion Effect: The Complete Guide.
157. Forms.app (2024). A full guide to the Pygmalion Effect to use in business.

www.ingramcontent.com/pod-product-compliance
Lightning Source LLC
Chambersburg PA
CBHW062141160726
48282CB00027B/899
9788197258107